Refreshing, inspiring, passionately written food for thought for days and years to come! The art enhances each message. This will be a keepsake as readers will learn, cherish, and continue our African-American heritage. Praise God for the visionaries, for those who taught and captured these lessons for the betterment of future generations.

DR. SHEILA BAILEY, Sheila B. Ministries

With *Our Help*, Our Daily Bread Ministries has provided a timeless treasure for the personal devotional life of justice-seeking Christians everywhere. In one tiny volume, this ample anthology packs writings from preachers, pastors, scholars, and Christian educators that inspire, encourage, and empower.

DR. TIMOTHY T. BODDIE, General Secretary,
Progressive National Baptist Convention

OUR HELP

DEVOTIONS ON STRUGGLE, VICTORY, LEGACY

JOYCE DINKINS AND
DIANE PROCTOR REEDER,
GENERAL EDITORS

Discovery House.
from Our Daily Bread Ministries

Our Help: Devotions on Struggle, Victory, Legacy
© 2018 by Matthew Parker

Discovery House is affiliated with Our Daily Bread Ministries, Grand Rapids, Michigan.

Articles by Lawrence Darmani, Joyce Dinkins, Xochitl E. Dixon, Arthur Jackson, David McCasland, Marvin A. McMickle and Marvin Williams © Our Daily Bread Ministries. Used by permission.

Requests for permission to quote from this book should be directed to: Permissions Department, Discovery House, PO Box 3566, Grand Rapids, MI 49501, or contact us by email at permissionsdept@dhp.org.

Cover design: Jan Spivey Gilchrist, Glynese Northam
Interior design: Glynese Northam

Library of Congress Cataloging-in-Publication Data

Names: Parker, Matthew, 1945- author.
Title: Our help : devotions on struggle, victory, legacy / by Matthew Parker.
Description: Grand Rapids : Discovery House, 2018. | Includes index.
Identifiers: LCCN 2017059592 | ISBN 9781627079013 (hardcover)
Subjects: LCSH: African Americans--Religion. | African Americans--Prayers and
    devotions.
Classification: LCC BR563.N4 P3855 2018 | DDC 277.3/08308996073--dc23
LC record available at https://lccn.loc.gov/2017059592

Printed in the United States of America
First printing in 2018

Contents

FOREWORD

The story of African-American struggle is familiar to our community, so much so that many African Americans express a kind of "fatigue" about hearing the oft-told stories of slavery and oppression. At the same time, we recognize that our history is important, and that we ignore it to our peril, because without it we fail to learn the rich lessons history has for us.

We also recognize that struggle and oppression do not form the totality of our story. We have had tremendous victories as well, with heroes and heroines well-known and obscure. We have those victors in our midst even today.

This book of devotionals weaves together struggle and victory within the African-American experience—including forty-five African-American writers who tell their own stories and put our history in its proper context—wrapped in a biblical perspective that brings wisdom and understanding for our daily Christian walk. We conclude with a set of legacy devotions that allow us to reflect on the vast richness of the African-American Christian experience over the centuries and generations.

Going from struggle to victory is not an easy road. It requires resisting feelings of failure and inadequacy. It requires a *mind renewal*, a global change of thinking. It requires the understanding that there is very little success that is accomplished without obstacles. Our obstacles will be of three sorts: the world (John 15:18), the flesh (Romans 7:22–23), and the devil (1 Peter 5:8). First of all, the devil does not want anyone to be successful in God's way. But if you have accepted the

Lord Jesus Christ and are walking in His will, He will be with you through every challenge in your life.

When you share God's will or vision of success with others, not everyone will support your dream. We can look in Genesis at the life of Joseph to see this. His beginning story is so similar to our ancestral story. His brothers not only did not support him; they hated him and sold him into slavery (Genesis 37:4–36). However, God was with him and made Joseph successful as a slave.

> The LORD was with Joseph so that he prospered, and he lived in the house of his Egyptian master. The blessing of the LORD was on everything Potiphar had, both in the house and in the field. So Potiphar left everything he had in Joseph's care; with Joseph in charge, he did not concern himself with anything except the food he ate (Genesis 39:2, 5–6 NIV).

Like many of our ancestors and even many of our contemporaries, Joseph became the victim of an unjust criminal justice system that sent him to prison for a crime he did not commit. Yet, God was with him and made him successful in prison (Genesis 39:7–23).

> But the LORD was with Joseph in the prison, and showed him his faithful love. And the LORD made Joseph a favourite with the prison warden. Before long, the warden put Joseph in charge of all the other prisoners and over everything that happened in the prison. The warden had no more worries, because Joseph took care of everything. The LORD was with him and caused everything he did to succeed (vv. 21–23).

Joseph was a man gifted with the interpretation of dreams, a gift he shared with his cellmates. He shared a dream with the king's cupbearer (trusted wine taster), so that the cupbearer would be freed. Thrilled about the prophecy, the cupbearer promised to tell Pharaoh about Joseph and see about getting Joseph released.

Sadly, the cupbearer forgot about Joseph in prison, but God brought Joseph back into his memory two years later:

> So Pharaoh sent for Joseph, and he was quickly brought from the dungeon (Genesis 41:14 NIV).

The Bible instructs us that our God-given personalities, abilities, and gifts can take us far. "Do you see someone skilled in their work? They will serve before kings; they will not serve before officials of low rank" (Proverbs 22:29 NIV). We see that in Joseph's story. After he interpreted Pharaoh's strange twin dreams, predicting a national famine and providing a wise plan to counter it, Pharaoh said to Joseph:

> "I hereby put you in charge of the whole land of Egypt." Then Pharaoh took his signet ring from his finger and put it on Joseph's finger. He dressed him in robes of fine linen and put a gold chain around his neck. He had him ride in a chariot as his second-in-command, and people shouted before him, "Make way!" Thus he put him in charge of the whole land of Egypt (Genesis 41:41–43 NIV).

This took place after seventeen years of obstacles; challenges; faith in God; spiritual, moral living; never giving up; and a positive attitude by Joseph for him to get from struggle to victory. Joseph lived a life of trusting. He trusted God for the rest of his life, leaving a rich legacy of faith, forgiveness, and service that was recorded for generations of Hebrews, and generations of people who would over the centuries give their lives to Jesus Christ.

> His brothers then came and threw themselves down before him. "We are your slaves," they said. But Joseph said to them, "Don't be afraid. Am I in the place of God? You intended to harm me, but God intended it for good to accomplish what is now being done, the saving of many lives. So then, don't be afraid. I will provide for you and your children." And he reassured them and spoke kindly to them (Genesis 50:18–21 NIV).

Sometimes, after failure, we are afraid that we will fail again. We do not doubt that Joseph had his own set of fears based on his circumstances; yet, he was confident in what God had given him, and he used his gift for good. It is good, therefore, for us to have confidence in what God has planted in us for our success; but it is more important for us to put our faith and confidence in the Lord:

> Have mercy on me, my God, have mercy on me, for in you I take refuge. I will take refuge in the shadow of your wings until the disaster has passed. I cry out to God Most High, to God, who vindicates [fulfills his purpose for] me (Psalm 57:1–2 NIV with author's note).

Matthew and *Matthew Parker*

Depend on God's Power

*They were registered by families—all the men of Israel
who were twenty years old or older and able to go to war.
The total number was 603,550.*
—Numbers 1:45–46

An *Umbundu* proverb from Angola says, *Unene wongandu
uli kovava*, meaning "the strength of the crocodile is
in the water." This proverb is used to explain that a leader's
power is found in the people. At first it seems like this proverb
agrees with the Bible. Moses and Aaron recorded the number
of warriors in each tribe and assigned leaders to them. The
leaders of Israel could not go to battle alone. They needed
all the fighting men to be successful—at least that was what
is often thought. But the victories of Israel were not in the
numerical strength of their army.

A crocodile is only as powerful as long as it is in the water.
Removed from the water, it is practically helpless. So it was
with Israel: Remove God from their midst and no matter how
many men went into battle, they would be defeated.

Israel brought the Tabernacle with them wherever they
went because that was where the Lord lived among his people (Numbers 1:50–53). As they conquered Canaan, the Lord
would fight for them as long as they obeyed him. As soon as
they disobeyed the Lord's commands, they found their power
was gone.

Just like Israel made God the centre of their lives, let us
make God the centre of ours. What battles are you facing that
you need to depend on God's power to help you with today?

—*Africa Study Bible* commentary on Numbers 1

PART ONE

JAN SPIVEY GILCHRIST

STRUGGLE

We've Come This Far

Breonna Rostic

"I have overcome the world."
John 16:33

Faith has brought us this far and we refuse to give up now
Although life has threatened to knock us out and flip us upside down
Cruel realities of this world snatched our dreams
and buried them in the ground
Faith has brought us this far and we refuse to give up now.

Distractions, disasters, disruptions nipping at our feet
Weighed down by guilt of not doing enough
and prayer burdens wearing on our knees
Haunted by the negative words that pierce
our soul—enough to scream
Starting to believe faith has brought us this far and that's enough
Until something stopped us in our tracks
like a deer enchanted by headlights
We were blind but now we see the struggles
were merely preparation for the victory.

We've become more than overcomers defeating
the monsters in our dreams
The seeds they once buried have now become full-grown trees
Bearing the fruit of the Spirit that will feed
our generations for centuries
Distractions strengthened our focus, disasters tested resolve,
and disruptions increased our patience
Because of them the problems of our future are already solved
Faith has brought us this far and that we can see
but our faith resides in the future we are yet to see.

*"We've Come This Far by Faith" is an
historic composition by Albert Goodson*

GENIUS

DIANE PROCTOR REEDER

*No, O people, the LORD has told you what is
good, and this is what he requires of you: to do
what is right, to love mercy, and to walk humbly
with your God.*

MICAH 6:8

I often think about our enslaved ancestors and the genius
behind their ability to learn the language of their oppres-
sors, and then learn "their" Bible . . . and then, miraculously,
take that book meant for their oppression and turn it into a
tool for liberation. Let's take a realistic and thoughtful look
at how that transformation occurred. For example, they
were spoon-fed the verse, "Slaves, obey your earthly masters"
(Ephesians 6:5), but then somehow God led them to Exodus
and the story of how He told Moses to demand freedom from
Egyptian rule for his people, the Hebrews. They were spoon-
fed the verse about obeying "authorities" (Hebrews 13:17
NIV), but then they heard the story of how Jesus turned over
tables in the Temple because He saw money-grubbing and
thievery (see Matthew 21:12–13).

And then it hits me: these people searched the Scriptures
for themselves. They often had to do it surreptitiously, as the
penalty to slaves for learning to read could be severe beating,
even death. Yet, they uncovered the untold stories of the Old
and New Testaments.

They heard and read verses about God being just: "And
shall not God avenge his own elect, which cry day and night
unto him?" (Luke 18:7 KJV). About mercy: "Let us fall

now into the hand of the LORD, for his mercies are great" (2 Samuel 24:14 KJV). They found themselves drawn to the God who was "touched with the feeling of our infirmities" (Hebrews 4:15 KJV). They were obedient to the command to "comfort them which are in any trouble, by the comfort wherewith we ourselves are comforted of God" (2 Corinthians 1:4 KJV).

They must have searched diligently. They must have searched faithfully. They must have searched extensively to find those precious verses and make for themselves a protective covering for their spirits, a covering given by God the Holy Spirit who indwelt them as they discovered the gospel message for themselves and then began to "work hard to show the results of [their own] salvation, obeying God with deep reverence and fear" (Philippians 2:12).

This is a *Selah* moment for me, a time to pause in awe of God and to think about what it took for these people who were so acted upon, so denigrated, yet were still able to learn, interpret, and apply Scripture to their harsh realities. It is a challenge moment for me to do the same thing, in God's strength.

REFLECTION:
How does this history inform your own desire to seek out the Scriptures and uncover their relevance for you today?

Suggested Scripture Reading: Exodus 9; Philippians 2:12

The Path of Promise

Shirley A. June

"The LORD himself will fight for you. Just stay calm."

Exodus 14:14

Can you remember a time when you felt you were "between a rock and a hard place"? If you have, you know it describes a situation that seems to have few or no possible options for a good outcome; a situation where it seems there is "no way out"!

Such were the nation of Israel's options as they journeyed through the wilderness from bondage in Egypt to the land of promise in Canaan. While camped, at God's direction, beside the sea, trouble came. They were in the will of God. They camped exactly where God instructed (Exodus 14:1, 9). Yet, they found themselves in a situation that threatened their freedom and survival, with Pharaoh's pursuing armies and chariots behind them and the sea before them. There was no safe place to turn.

Their journey had started out with high expectations but they quickly turned to desperation. "Why did you bring us out here to die in the wilderness," they bitterly complained (Exodus 14:11). "Let us be slaves to the Egyptians!" (v. 12). Returning to Egypt and slavery seemed a better alternative to the death and destruction they seemed to be facing.

How quickly they forgot: God had started them out on this journey, and He would be able to see them through.

We, like they, sometimes get distracted because of difficulties along the path of promise. Sometimes the greatest threats are prelude to the sure victories God has planned. God alone knows the full meaning of our situation, and how it fits with His overall plan and our destiny. We, on the other hand, may misjudge what God is doing in our lives and the reason for our plight or dilemma. We wonder why and voice our complaint, *I'm praying. I'm fasting. I'm reading my Word. Why doesn't God hear me? Doesn't He see my situation?*

However it may seem, the safest place to be is in the will of God. Wherever our life goes, we have to be clear: we have not traveled this way before, but God knows the way. Even more, He *is* the way (John 14:6). He moves us from fear to faith. And He will always be our "refuge and strength, an ever-present help in trouble" (Psalm 46:1 NIV).

REFLECTION:
When you think about turning away from your faith—from your submission to and obedience to God—what instead do you think about turning to? What would be the cost?

Suggested Scripture Reading: Psalm 91

A Father's Forgiveness

Arthur Jackson

*See how very much our Father loves us, for he
calls us his children, and that is what we are!*

1 JOHN 3:1

When a judge's pronouncement of multiple life sentences echoed through the courtroom, "two deaths" were mourned. A college-age son had been murdered; the young man and a friend were gunned down as they innocently played video games at another friend's home. The young man's heavy-hearted father was present that day for the sentencing hearing. But the pangs of grief that gnawed at the father were not only for the son he had lost. He was deeply disturbed because another young man—with most of his years before him—was headed to prison for the remainder of his days. The anguished father was left to struggle with loss and hopelessness.

Courtroom confusion and angst eventually yielded to compassionate action as the father found his heart drawn miraculously to the young man who had taken his son's life. He began writing the young convict. He had no way to know that his son's killer had begun to yearn for some sign to assure him that "God is real." Over time, the father mustered up enough courage to request a personal visit with his son's killer, and it was arranged.

The anxiety that attended the anticipated encounter gave way to genuine joy as the two men, who were joined together by horrifying tragedy, embraced each other and wept. The two developed an authentic, loving relationship. The father calls the young man who took his son's life "his son"; and the one who took that life calls the deceased son's father "his dad."

The forgiveness of God is the heartbeat of the Christian message. Titus 3:3–7 packages this good news. God's love and kindness appeared in living color in the person of Jesus Christ (v. 4) whose death was a payment for the forgiveness of sins— spiritual cleansing (v. 5). Because of the overflowing mercy of God, unlovely people (v. 3) can become members of God's eternal family (v. 7).

Each of us who receives the forgiveness of God through Jesus has a "forgiveness story." People who are offensive to God and others because of selfish, sinful rebellion are brought into the family of God through forgiveness. We are no longer under the sentence of condemnation. Rather, we are gripped to the point of wonder and worship because "the forgiveness of God" through the Lord Jesus Christ is the grand theme of our lives.

Father, we are humbled by Your forgiveness that
brings those who are far away from You
into Your family.

REFLECTION:
Do you have a story of your own about experiencing or witnessing unbelievable forgiveness?

Suggested Scripture Reading: Titus 3:4–7;
see also 1 John 3:1–3

Knowing Your Enemy

Patricia Raybon

For we are not fighting against flesh-and-blood enemies, but against evil rulers and authorities of the unseen world, against mighty powers in this dark world, and against evil spirits in the heavenly places.

Ephesians 6:12

The line at the five-and-dime store was quiet but mighty. A picket line. Protesters with signs urged a boycott of the downtown Woolworth's store in my hometown of Denver. I was a preteen then and Woolworth's was a favorite hangout. I went there with friends to splurge our meager allowance money on apple pie, ice cream, popcorn, and sodas. Cheap, bad food. Much worse, however, in this Jim Crow era, were segregation rules across the South that barred "Negroes" like my friends and me from even sitting in Woolworth's at a "whites only" lunch counter.

The insult assaulted Negro dignity, but also national principles. Therefore, young black college students in North Carolina staged a sit-in protest at a Woolworth's store in Greensboro on February 1, 1960. Heroes to some, the students faced ridicule from others who argued their right to be served a snack was "small potatoes" and wouldn't change much.

But the students knew their real enemy: racial discrimination, a scourge fueled by Satan himself. As civil rights leader Ella Baker explained, the sit-ins were "concerned with something more than a hamburger." Added activist Dick Gregory,

"This isn't a revolution of black against white; this is a revolution of right against wrong."

Such moral clarity should inspire spiritual warriors today. "For our struggle is not against flesh and blood," wrote the apostle Paul, "but against the rulers, against the authorities, against the powers of this dark world and against the spiritual forces of evil in the heavenly realms" (Ephesians 6:12 NIV).

Fighting such evil, the Greensboro sit-in struck a national nerve. Within three months, sit-ins were staged in more than 55 US cities in 13 states. It was "love in action," declared the Reverend Dr. Martin Luther King Jr. in an interview with Robert Penn Warren. Therefore, it was not about hating storeowners, but "loving them so much" you're "willing to sit in at a lunch counter in order to help them find themselves," King said.

The result? Not only did the F. W. Woolworth Company reverse its racist policies, but lunch-counter protests helped establish the US Civil Rights Movement as an unstoppable force.

Back in Denver, I joined the fight in my own way. I refused to cross that Woolworth's picket line. A friend teased me, urging, "Let's just go inside and eat!"

But I could see what the marchers were battling—Satan's lie that blacks were inferior. To help fight that blight, I pulled on courage and honored the boycott. The lesson learned? Know your enemy. Then God leads His people to win every time.

REFLECTION:
In your life, if you're facing a struggle, can you name your real enemy?

Suggested Scripture Reading: Matthew 16:21–23; Ephesians 6:11–13

The Wounded Healer

George Dallas McKinney

*But he was wounded for our transgressions, he
was bruised for our iniquities: the chastisement
of our peace was upon him; and with his stripes
we are healed.*

Isaiah 53:5 KJV

During the turbulent sixties, under the ministry of Dr. Martin Luther King Jr., we learned that "undeserved suffering is redemptive." Dr. King was saying that in the non-violent struggle for justice, equality, and community, the truth that Jesus proclaimed centuries before was demonstrated: one person can stand in the place of and take on the suffering of another. And, through the suffering of the righteous, the unrighteous can be made righteous.

We learned then, through the suffering of the young people who were willing to be arrested and to endure cruel beatings and attacks from dogs simply because they stood up for brotherhood and justice, that God moved in a mighty way and turned a whole nation around. God took the suffering of a few to heal the wounds of many.

We have a clear statement in God's Word in the "Suffering Servant" chapter, Isaiah 53, regarding the vicarious sacrifice of Jesus Christ. In it, we see a picture of Jesus as He suffered, died, and rose again for all of our sickness and disease. He is portrayed as the Sufferer, who was beaten, bruised, falsely arrested, taken from one judgment hall to another, and finally crucified. He died, made His grave with the wicked, and was buried in a wealthy man's tomb, just as the prophet said (vv. 3–9).

He who knew no sin, He in whom was found no guile, He who was faultless, assumed faults, bore our sins, took upon Himself our sickness and disease, that we might be healed (v. 5).

When trials surround us, we should flee to God and confidently expect help from Him who is mighty to save and strong to deliver. "Many are the afflictions of the righteous, but the Lord delivers him out of them all" (Psalm 34:19 NKJV).

Open the windows of the soul heavenward, and let the light of the Son of Righteousness in. Deliverance can come by letting the peace of God reign in your soul. Then you will have strength to bear all your sufferings, and you will rejoice that you have grace to endure. Praise the Lord; talk of His goodness; tell of His power. Sweeten the atmosphere that surrounds your soul.

Whatever may be your circumstances, the assurance still comes. "And we know that God causes everything to work together for the good of those who love God and are called according to his purpose for them" (Romans 8:28). "I know whom I have believed, and am persuaded that he is able to keep that which I have committed unto him against that day" (2 Timothy 1:12 KJV).

We need to cultivate gratitude. We should frequently contemplate and recount the mercies of God, and laud and glorify His holy name even when we are passing through sorrow and affliction. Being a Christian does not exempt one from affliction, but gives strength to endure.

REFLECTION:
God delivers in this life, and completely in the life to come.

Suggested Scripture Reading: Isaiah 53; Romans 8

LEARNING TO WALK IN THE DARK

VICTORIA SAUNDERS MCAFEE

The LORD directs the steps of the godly. He delights in every detail of their lives.

PSALM 37:23

In 1894, Mary McLeod Bethune attended Moody Bible Institute; she was the only African-American student. She hoped to become a missionary to Africa, but her application was denied because of her "race." Mary returned to her hometown in South Carolina, disappointed and feeling like a failure.

However, years later, God allowed Mrs. Bethune to open a Christian school in Florida, which is now Bethune-Cookman University. Instead of sending one person, Mary, overseas, God sent and is still sending hundreds of students from the college as Christian workers all over the US and around the world. God redirected Mrs. Bethune in order to reach more people for His kingdom.

The apostle Paul often experienced God's redirection. On one occasion, he planned to go to Asia, but the Holy Spirit said no. He arranged travel to Bithynia, but once again the Spirit blocked his path. Then he experienced a vision instructing him to go to Macedonia. There he found Lydia and a small group of women (Acts 16:6–14). This gathering birthed the Philippian church, which grew and became very influential for Christ. God intercepted Paul's plans, resulting in greater fruitfulness.

Redirection is hard. We get discouraged, frustrated, and even angry as we ask, *Where are you leading me, Lord? The road is dark, and the signs I'm seeing along the way are confusing.*

God responds, "Be patient, persevere, draw close to Me, trust Me and not yourself" (see Proverbs 3:5–6).

> "In each experience of my life, I have had to step out of one little space of the known light, into a large area of darkness. I had to stand awhile in the darkness, and then gradually God has given me light. But not to linger in. For as soon as that light has felt familiar, then the call has always come to step out ahead again into new darkness."
>
> MARY MCLEOD BETHUNE

Lord, I thought You were wanting me over here;
now that door is closed. What's going on?
Please, teach me to trust You, even in the dark.

REFLECTION:
Have you ever questioned God? Have you ever made a conscious decision to "step again into new darkness"?

Suggested Scripture Reading: Psalm 37:3–5; 23–34

If I Had My Way

David Salmon

Then the LORD God called to the man, "Where are you?"

GENESIS 3:9

I boarded the plane and prepared for the 11-hour flight to Tokyo, Japan. Slumping into my seat with an air of selfish entitlement, I thought, *I have made these journeys too many times before! If I had my way, I wouldn't be here.*

As a navy man, I began my marriage often traveling away from my wife aboard ship. I made wrong decisions, dishonoring God, my wife, and my marital vows. Mercifully, God humbled me and helped me to submit my "dead" life to Him through Christ. He forgave me. My bride did too. We have now been married for more than 48 years at this writing, and we help other couples get—or keep—their marriages on track.

So there I sat on an aircraft, not relishing my absence away from my wife and family, and thinking about her possibly worrying about my whereabouts. I found myself muttering, "If I had my way, I wouldn't be here."

Instantly, God impressed on me—speaking as He is known to do when dealing with one of His shortsighted, complaining children: *It's true: if you had had your way, you wouldn't be here.* And in the quiet of the next few moments, He allowed me to ponder the depth and breadth of that truth and its realities.

I thought about all that God had done to bring me through the mess I had made in my life, and about the fact that I am still married to a beautiful Christian woman. I am a father to three great children, gainfully employed, and trusted to represent the Lord Jesus as a Christian man. Humbled, tears of thanksgiving flowed from my eyes, and I wrote:

> If I'd had my way, I wouldn't be here,
> But I thank God that isn't the case.
> For He knew my heart and He knew my condition,
> And He reached down and saved me by His grace.
>
> For I was bound for hell, completely lost in my sin
> But this Sovereign God gave me new life with Him.
>
> So you see, so you see, so you see,
> If I'd had my way, I wouldn't be here,
> But I thank God for His grace.

God has now broadened for me what it means to be "here"; my life means exponentially more than just being where *I* want to be. "Here" is to know Christ Jesus and to live "in Him," acknowledging His presence in every way.

> *Lord, I just want to be where You are, doing*
> *what You want me to do. That is enough for*
> *me. In Jesus's name, amen.*

REFLECTION:
If you are grateful that you didn't have your way, thank God! If there is a place where you wish you were, ask Him what your next step should be.

Suggested Scripture Reading: Proverbs 14:1–15

QUESTIONS

DIANE PROCTOR REEDER

*Call to me and I will answer you and tell you
great and unsearchable things you do not know.*
JEREMIAH 33:3

When you are "in it," wondering why you have to suffer, questions pound your soul. This happened to me, not when my husband died after a four-year battle with leukemia, but two years later, when my otherwise hale and healthy father died very suddenly after a seeming bout with food poisoning.

If you're wise, you seek counsel. You ask questions. And sometimes the well-meaning counsel comes back: "Don't question God. He knows what's best." But when we go back and read the ancient stories of the Old Testament, one of the best lessons is that those who were *closest* to God *asked* questions.

"Should not the Judge of all the earth do what is right?" Abraham asks God (Genesis 18:25), begging Him not to kill the righteous along with the wicked of the city of Sodom. "Can the dead live again?" asks Job (Job 14:14), in the midst of his so-called friends who tried to connect his suffering to his sin. (Note that they never asked God anything.) "What is his [Your] name?" asked Moses of God (Exodus 3:13), seeking ways to answer the stubborn people he was leading. Then the plaintive cry of the prophet Habakkuk, "How long, O LORD, must I call for help? But you do not listen!" (Habakkuk 1:2).

That is the question, isn't it? "How long, Lord?"

Yet some pesky counselor may warn us against questioning God. Spook us with unwarranted fears. So we keep our questions to ourselves.

God never intended that. Instead, He invites us into dialogue. "Come, have dinner with me," says Jesus to us. "Open the door to my knock, and let's eat together" (Revelation 3:20, paraphrased). What do we do when we eat together? We talk!

These towering figures—Moses; Abraham; Job; and David, who was called a "friend of God"—all asked questions. And God answered them! When Moses asked, "What is his [Your] name," God told him, "I AM " (Exodus 3:14). When Abraham begged God to change His mind about killing all the Sodomites, He did (Genesis 18:32). God's answer to Habakkuk was about a painful conquest to come, but He at least told him the truth (Habakkuk 1:5–6).

We can always ask God our questions. That reflects deep intimacy. We need to be ready for the answer . . . and for questions God asks us. He may ask, as He did Adam, "Where are you?" (Genesis 3:9). Or, He may challenge, as Jesus did when He asked, "For what shall it profit a man, if he shall gain the whole world, and lose his own soul?" (Mark 8:36 KJV).

Questions are evidence not of doubt, but of our faith. God wants us to engage Him. To do that, how can we avoid asking questions? But be forewarned: He will respond with more questions, including the most important, the one Jesus asked Peter the disciple: "But who do you say I am?" (Mark 8:29).

REFLECTION:
List your God-questions. Offer them up to Him in prayer. See how He answers. Preserve, possibly in a journal.

Suggested Scripture Reading: Psalm 17:6; Jeremiah 33:3; Matthew 16:15

Running in the Wrong Direction

Victoria Saunders McAfee

*He said, "In my distress I called to the Lord, and
he answered me, from deep in the realm of the
dead I called for help, and you listened to my cry."*
JONAH 2:2

My son joined a Pee Wee Football League team when he
was about six years old. At one of his games his team-
mate caught the football. The little guy tucked that football
in his arm and took off running. He was so excited. Sadly, he
ran in the wrong direction. He ran with all his might toward
the opposite team's goalpost. The coach, his parents, all of
us in the audience shouted and screamed, "Wrong way, turn
around!" But he was focused on getting to that goal line. The
coach ran down the field to deliver the disappointing news,
"You just scored a touchdown for the wrong team!"

Ever done that? Picked up the ball of your fleshly desires,
a worldly ambition, or one of Satan's well-crafted lies and
then ran in the wrong direction? The Father, Son, Holy Spirit,
wise Christian friends, and your own guilty conscience were
all shouting and screaming from the sidelines something like
this: "You are going the wrong way; bad choice; you are about
to score one for Satan's kingdom; stop, turn around, think
this through." But sometimes we've got our self-centered,
I-got-this talk covering our ears. We refuse to listen.

We'd like to think this kind of running in the wrong
direction only happens to new Christians, or those who are
immature. Yet even those who've been walking with the Lord
for a while, knee-deep in ministry, can get turned around.

The Bible is filled with God's children who at one time (or several times) got turned around. Abraham got his wife's handmaiden Hagar pregnant instead of waiting on God's timing with Sarah (Genesis 16:1–4). Or the famous case of Jonah: God told him where to go and he took a ship going the *opposite* direction (Jonah 1:1–3). In each case, the parties involved suffered consequences, affecting them personally and sometimes their loved ones.

The story you just read has a good news ending. You see, when the coach explained to his young player what he'd done he burst into tears. The wise coach swept him up in his arms, set him down on the bench, bent down on one knee and looked the little boy straight in the eye. "Wipe your face," he said. "Rest up, get ready for the next play; we need you, and the game is not over."

How many times has God had to swoop up one of His children into His arms, wipe tears away, give a "pep talk," and put us back in the game of life? We may want to quit, but He forgives. His grace and mercy extend long and deep. He gives us another chance . . . and another. He lovingly lets us know, *You are still in the game; you are still valuable to Me. The game is not over.*

REFLECTION:

When is the last time you found yourself in "the belly of a whale"? Going the wrong direction? What did you say to yourself? What did God say to you? How did you get turned around?

Suggested Scripture Reading: Jonah 2:1–10

Armed and Ready

Arthur Jackson

We use God's mighty weapons, not worldly weapons.

2 Corinthians 10:4

When you think of the word *weapon*, what other word or image comes to mind? The most natural answer for many of us is *gun*. This is true whether you live in an urban community, a remote area, in the suburbs, or even at a resort. People in our communities know all too much about too many weapons that have destroyed or taken too many lives. We mourn the loss of innocent children and others; we also lament the fact that those who commit crimes will be lost through incarceration.

Thankfully, weapons that harm others are not the only kind. Desiring to make the most of my time when I accompanied my wife to a doctor's appointment, I took my Bible so I could read while waiting. Entering the building, I heard these words: "Sir, you know they don't allow weapons in the building." I was taken aback a bit and casually commented that I had no weapon. The thought-provoking words of the building attendant let me know that she recognized that the book I was carrying relates to God's dynamic power.

God's Word is the most powerful *spiritual* weapon. God provides safety for those who put their trust in Him. Appropriately, God refers to *armor* (Ephesians 6:11), and safeguarding of the whole person is in view—from head to toe. Included in the list of what God gives is "the sword of the Spirit, which is the word of God" (Ephesians 6:17). We must ask ourselves if we are prepared to skillfully wield this most important spiritual weapon.

Growing up, my spiritual education included the formal and informal instruction of a grandmother in the home and church mothers and other godly people at our humble church. I fondly recall the cake that my brother and I were awarded when we memorized the books of the Bible. Oh, how our communities need those who will labor with our children and youth and instill in them the value of God's Word. This kind of investment will prepare them to resist the opposing forces they will face in this world.

The experience of Jesus in the wilderness is a classic example of the usefulness of Scripture when temptations come our way. When tempted to abandon His God-appointed mission, Jesus quoted Scripture from memory, stood His ground, and was strengthened (Matthew 4:1–11).

The practical usefulness of Scripture must not be underestimated. When pressured with thoughts, feelings, and temptations that contradict our convictions and threaten our well-being, Scripture in our hearts arms us for battle and readies us for life.

*Father, help me to be aware of the power of
Your Word and to use it for my soul's
good and the good of others!*

REFLECTION:
What are key Scriptures or life verses for you?

Suggested Scripture Reading: 2 Corinthians 10:3–6;
Ephesians 6:10–20

Hate—or Pain?

Diane Proctor Reeder

Three things will last forever—faith, hope and
love—and the greatest of these is love.

1 Corinthians 13:13

The brilliant author James Baldwin, son of a preacher, wrote frequently about issues around racism. And while he seemed to deny his Christian faith as an adult, the fruit of his exposure to the Scriptures as a child and adolescent often seep through his eloquent prose. In one of the essays penned in his book, *Notes of a Native Son*, Baldwin writes:

> "I imagine that one of the reasons people cling to their hates so stubbornly is because they sense, once hate is gone, that they will be forced to deal with pain."

We continue to witness the hate of racism and injustice. We who hold fast to new life and the human equality God intended for us according to His Word watch in horror at recurring racially motivated events of hatred. We even witness some who drape themselves in religious rhetoric to masquerade as Christians while expressing hatred. It may make us wonder: *What is going on? Why the anger? Why anger directed at people many of them have never even met?* We grieve and wonder if there will ever be a time when we move forward in a straight line without seeming to continuously go backward in the critical area of human relations.

But as God's Word tells us, "Nothing under the sun is truly new" (Ecclesiastes 1:9). Everything old is only new to subsequent generations.

How do Christians address the backlash of hate that seems to hit others in the news and us in our own lives every day? With resistance, most assuredly. But do we *dare* to meet hate with love? And what does that look like, both to the hated and to the haters? The wise Solomon instructs us that "Love is as strong as death" (Song of Solomon 8:6). Strong indeed.

How might Christians be called to respond in uncertain and often cruel times?

We pray and believe that love will be strong enough for us to weather the times in which we find ourselves.

REFLECTION:
How do we live with God's love in mind? Ask God, *How's my living looking?*

Suggested Scripture Reading: 1 Corinthians 13

Straight Outta Nazareth

Michael Lyles

Can anything good come out of Nazareth?
John 1:46 (NKJV)

Nathanael, the disciple to whom this quote is attributed, was a cynical sort. There was a reason he sneered when Philip invited him to come and see the One whom "the prophets wrote about!" (John 1:45).

Nazareth is known as Jesus's hometown and nothing else. He was born in Bethlehem (Matthew 2:1–5; Luke 2:1–7) but was raised in Nazareth. That was a small town of about 400 people, mainly laborers. There was nothing fancy; it was *not* a "destination location." There was a Roman military installation nearby, which further decreased property values, so to speak. Who wanted to live near a military base of soldiers who disrespected Jews? Affluent Jews would live near the big city of Jerusalem, not in this piece of a town. No wonder Nathanael had such a prejudice about people from Nazareth.

Detroit's east side was my "Nazareth." Very few people had any positive expectations of anyone coming out of the east side. We were expected to fail at school, consume drugs, assault each other, and have babies outside of marriage. No one would hire me for a summer job washing dishes in a restaurant because "you can't trust people from 'Nazareth.'" *They will steal or not show up for work on time.* My "Nazareth" friends drank the drink about "Nazareth." They thought that the only ways "outta Nazareth" were to play sports, sing, or get an illegal hustle like gambling—"playing the numbers"— or drug dealing.

It's bad enough when you are *from* "Nazareth." It's worse when the stereotypes and lies about "Nazareth" get *inside* you. My friends were harsh on themselves and, one by one, too many of them self-destructed.

God had every option for where Jesus could have grown up as a human being. He could have had the prophets predict that He would grow up in a nice, prosperous neighborhood. Instead, He chose Nazareth. Jesus would model that God could make something really good come "straight outta Nazareth."

If we let Him be, He is bigger than any of our "Nazareths"; not limited by bias, racism, stereotypes, and bigotry. God did not care that some people did not like Jesus because He was from Nazareth. Take your clue from Him, and consider the very human predictions and expectations of others to be just that: *human*. And consider instead how He has chosen you, and elevated you to the "royal priesthood" by virtue of His death on the cross (1 Peter 2:9). That does not depend on your *geography*, but on your *spiritual* position in Him . . . and that is something to shout about!

REFLECTION:
What is the "Nazareth" that is limiting what I think that God can do with my life?

Suggested Scripture Reading: Hebrews 4:14–16

All Things?

NORVELLA CARTER

And we know that God causes everything to work together for the good of those who love God and are called according to his purpose for them.

ROMANS 8:28

My husband and I grew impatient one Sunday morning while listening to a visiting pastor preach at our son's morning church service. We were visitors, too, and felt a little disappointed that we chose a Sunday when the official pastor was away. The sermon that morning was based on Romans 8:28. He repeated the phrase "all things" multiple times and gave examples of circumstances that "all things" encompassed. Some, we thought, were gruesome. His goal was to emphasize that any circumstance we face as Christians will be transformed into something good according to His purpose for us, and we need to trust God to do so.

Within months of that sermon, our daughter, Tracie, who was successfully battling breast cancer, suddenly passed away. Our son, William, who was a captain in the US Army and studying to be a chaplain, spoke a powerful and uplifting message at her funeral service. A few days later, William, while preparing to return to Iraq for a second tour of military duty, succumbed to an unexpected virus and passed away. In less than two weeks, my husband and I suffered the loss of two children. *All things. Really?*

Both Tracie and William loved the Lord and had ministries making an impact in their families and in multiple communities. So, we knew then and we know now, they are with the Lord. Still, we suffered intense pain and sorrow. In the midst of our grief, we remembered the Bible words the visiting pastor recounted: "All things work together for good . . . all things . . . all things . . . all things." The words rang painfully in our heads.

We were faced with the challenge of sincerely believing the Word of God, trusting it to be true, and applying it to our personal lives. It was a real struggle for us. We understood Lamentations 3:22–23, which says, "It is of the LORD's mercies that we are not consumed, because his compassions fail not. They are new every morning: great is thy faithfulness" (KJV). We had to trust the Lord daily for His mercy, to get through the gripping days and the tearful nights. We had to trust the Lord's sovereignty and decisions about life and death. Regardless of our feelings, we had to trust that everything, even the deaths of our dear children, would be transformed into something good.

It has been ten years since the deaths of Tracie and William. Among our 15 grandchildren are grandson Trace and grandson William, namesakes of their aunt and uncle. Little by little, the Lord turned our sorrow into joy. We can now testify to others that we do not grieve as others "who have no hope" (1 Thessalonians 4:13).

We remember that visiting pastor fondly. I believe he was ministering directly into our souls for the days that would come. All things. . . .

REFLECTION:
When the worst happens, what are the verses that most comfort your soul?

Suggested Scripture Reading: Lamentations 3:22–23

COME AND REST

RESNA MARIE BRUNSON

"Come to me, all you who are weary and carry heavy burdens, and I will give you rest."
MATTHEW 11:28

When my girls were little, I could encourage them to take naps by telling them, "Princesses need beauty rest." A nap can revive and refresh us from our struggles. Circumstances may remain the same, but somehow we seem to think clearer and are more hopeful when we are well rested.

But I remember a time when I felt like David, who, when his life was in grave danger, said, "Oh, that I had wings like a dove; then I would fly away and rest!" (Psalm 55:6). I was tired of being tired and could not see a way out. The Lord was calling out to me, but I was not in tune with Him. For days I felt as though the walls of my life were caving in. I had allowed my circumstances to overshadow His presence. I was not listening to His voice. After realizing only He could help me, I opened my devotional book and there was the passage "Come to me, all you who are weary and burdened, and I will give you rest" (Matthew 11:28 NIV). The Lord had been nudging me; now He was calling, as it were, from the rooftops! I had to listen. I had to rest in Him.

When we allow Him to lead us to this resting place, God promises a yoke that is light and rest for our souls (see Matthew 11:29–30).

We all have burdens: family issues, work, school, financial concerns. . . . At times the weight is overwhelming. But God promises if we come to Him and take on His way of love, joy, forgiveness, and humility, our burdens (although still present) will be light.

There are times, however, when we want to rest in the Lord but hindrances stand in our way, including unconfessed sin. I can think of instances where Satan used guilt and shame to deceive and cripple me. I thought I was unworthy of God's blessings, when the problem was I simply needed to repent. Conversely, when I stay " 'fessed up," I feel unashamed to go to Him in "time of need"—at all times—and to spend quality time meditating and resting on His Word.

This is the good news: God loves us with an everlasting, unconditional love, demonstrated to us by His death on the cross. Restlessness leads to anxiety and a heavy heart. But that is not God's intention for us. No matter what the circumstance, God is still navigating the situation for our good and His glory. We rest knowing that He is in control. He never promised to take all difficult circumstances away, but we rest knowing He is omniscient and always ready to bear our burdens.

Are we willing to take God at His word? Are we ready to release those burdens? The heavenly Father is calling us to rest in Him.

REFLECTION:
When was the last time you truly rested in the Lord?

Suggested Scripture Reading: Matthew 11:28–30;
John 1:1–16

SECOND CHANCE SECURITY

DIANE PROCTOR REEDER

He led me to a place of safety; he rescued me
because he delights in me.

PSALM 18:19

When my husband died, I prepared for the funeral by, among other things, getting my hair done. The trip to the hairdresser was bittersweet; I would no longer come home to a man who would always say when I came back from the hairdresser, "Nice!" and raise his eyebrows in appreciation. It was a small but painful realization.

As I sat in the chair, getting my hair pulled back from my face with extra hair woven into a fancy bun—I wanted the morning of his funeral to be an "easy hair day"—I listened to the chatter of the beauticians. A woman getting her hair done commented that she liked mine. I did too. The one doing my hair, not my usual beautician, said "Yes, a lot of the widows do their hair like this."

Ouch. Is that what I am now? And is this the end of "life as I know it"?

That was more than 17 years ago. I found out that did not have to be the end. There is, after all, life after everything.

This year I read in *Prayers of a Young Poet* by Rainer Maria Rilke:

> I love the dark hours of my being, for they deepen my
> senses.
>
> From them I've come to know that I have room
> for a second life, timeless and wide.

And I realized once again with gratefulness that God is even in the dark, deepening my dependence on Him, setting me up for another kind of life, different but satisfying and joyous. You see, the darkness and the light are alike to Him. He sees in the dark, so we don't have to (Psalm 139:12).

I stand in Him today a grateful woman. Grateful for blessings, even when they are masked in what seem to be curses. Grateful that, just as He knit me together in my mother's womb and created my inmost being, He has knit together my circumstances into a life-tapestry unique and specially designed for me, to allow me to live out His rich purposes for me. I am secure in His "spacious" love for me (Psalm 139:13 NIV).

Gratefulness is flowing from my heart.

REFLECTION:
Are you secure in the fact that God sees you? Do you see God's purposes in your life, including during suffering? What do you think He is positioning you for?

Suggested Scripture Reading: Psalm 139:1–15

DEFEATING ADDICTIONS

CLARENCE SHULER

I will refuse to look at anything vile and vulgar.
PSALM 101:3

Talk about struggle; addictions plague many people. I was addicted to pornography for 11 years. Any person can get stuck in a cycle of temptation, yielding, and immediately feeling guilty, asking for forgiveness, but not feeling forgiven or clean. And always feeling unworthy, even hypocritical. But continuing in that cycle over and over again.

Those addicted, whether to pornography or another addictive behavior, are not alone or forsaken by God. I've been clean for twenty-three years at this writing. What was once my *misery* is now my *ministry*.

For me, gaining the victory over my struggle came through truly incorporating God's principles in my life each day. First and foremost was admitting that I was addicted and could not stop my sin. Confession to God brings light to sin done in darkness and weakens any addiction's hold on most people. Having a devotional time with God daily also can help those who struggle with addictions. I also had to get a trustworthy person to help hold me accountable. Experts can provide other helps, depending on the struggle.

Any addiction has an impact also on our family, friends, and on our spiritual legacy. God will always forgive us for sin, though we'll always suffer consequences. The devil does not tell us all of that when he entices us.

Above all, our thinking and behavior must match God's truth, not human emotions. "I made a covenant with my eyes

45

not to look with lust" (Job 31:1) is the basis for giving up pornographic and other lustful behavior. The more we say no to addictive temptations and yes to the truth of God's Word, the easier it becomes to overcome—and our emotions will catch up with our actions. But our emotions won't change without our actions changing.

Thankfully, prayer helps us change. "Lord, free me from my addiction and anything I do in conjunction with my addiction. Please let the indwelling Holy Spirit's power, Your Word's encouragement, and the accountability to my friend help me take captive every thought that isn't honoring to You (see 2 Corinthians 10:5). Help me defeat my addiction. I want to experience Your sweet fellowship and to be a clean vessel You can use for Your glory!"

God has given us the power to defeat addictions through the person of the indwelling Holy Spirit. Yielding to the Spirit's guidance, we can remember that God loves us! According to Psalm 139:14, God calls us marvelous! Each of His children is special and can have a godly destiny. We can do all things through Christ, who'll strengthen us to apply the discipline we need in our struggle to defeat our addictions (Philippians 4:13).

God, I want peace and oneness with You through Jesus Christ.

REFLECTION:
You can make godly choices each day, all day long.

Suggested Scripture Reading: Psalm 101:2–3; Romans 12:1–2

In a Box

Anita Patterson

This hope is a strong and trustworthy anchor for our souls. It leads us through the curtain into God's inner sanctuary.

HEBREWS 6:19

It's bad enough to be in a box. It's worse when your box is out thrashing at sea.

I was with my mother in the emergency room at one hospital. At another, my brother was having heart surgery. Two hospitals, two people I loved, both in critical condition on the same day. I wept aloud to the Lord in my distress. "What should I do? Who should I go to the hospital to be with?"

God spoke out of His Word. "Be strong and of a good courage," He told me. I dried my eyes and listened. I had to speak about God's power to myself just as David had (1 Samuel 30:6). *I will be strong, wait, listen, trust in God and be of good courage,* I told myself. *I will be brave and unmovable, standing firmly on God's Word and promises.*

Mother and brother are here today, and both are just fine, thankfully. Importantly, God was with us in our struggles.

At times, circumstances can make us feel hopeless, helpless, and lifeless. *Where is God? Why doesn't He do something about my pain, misery and disappointment . . . and why doesn't He do it now?* we ask ourselves.

In 1 Samuel 30:6, David found himself in a situation. His men wanted to stone him; the very men that served with him in battle. They went to fight their enemies on David's direction, saw their wives and children taken captive, and wept before the Lord. They then blamed David for their calamity.

David was boxed in, and his box shook on the turbulent waters. In his agony, he went to a place where he knew he could get help, encouragement, and comfort. He called on the Lord Jesus in his anguish. He did not simply consult with friends on social media. He didn't have a pity party. He didn't call a psychic, or instruct them to go ahead and kill him. David knew his relationship with God was solid and he could depend on God for wisdom and strength. Even during all of the madness, he anchored down, trusting and believing God to deliver him out of circumstances and save his life. God saved David, his men, and all of their families.

When you find yourself in a box, anchor down in the Word of God. Wait for Him to strengthen you and uphold you amid the turbulence.

Lord, help me to seek You, anchor down in Your Word, and rely on You during difficult and uncertain situations.

REFLECTION:
Have you ever found yourself in a situation where you felt like you were in a box closing in on you or tossing around in a stormy sea of circumstances? What do you normally do when that happens?

Suggested Scripture Reading: 1 Samuel 30:6; Hebrews 6:16–19

Overcoming Adversity

Cheri Perron

*"For I know the plans I have for you," declares
the* Lord, *"plans to prosper you and not to harm
you, plans to give you hope and a future."*

Jeremiah 29:11 niv

When traumatic events happen in our lives we often wonder, *Where is God? Why did He allow it to happen? Why didn't He stop it?* When we delve into the lives of prominent Christians—ones we may admire and even envy—we have to rethink our assumptions. Author of the Power of Praying series, Stormie Omartian was a victim of abuse. Hymnist Horatio Spafford wrote the lyrics for "It Is Well with My Soul" after the tragic loss of all five of his children. Christian author and artist Joni Eareckson Tada wrote and painted works to lift millions of people, but only after she became a quadriplegic. These individuals walked through adversity and overcame traumatic events as they trusted God.

What was their secret? They refused to be victimized. They chose to use their past struggles to bless and teach others how to overcome. In order to heal from the past, we have to face the pain of the past; knowing that healing can begin at the point of pain. Jeremiah's plaintive cry, "O Lord, if you heal me, I will be truly healed" (Jeremiah 17:14), is at once a prayer and an assertive, confident affirmation of God's sufficiency.

We learn to accept these situations as part of a world of sin and its results. And we believe that God, in His wisdom and power, can cause the pain we experience to serve His great purpose.

We don't know what God has planned for our lives; we have limited insight. But God, as the Master of our lives, knows, controls, and sees all (1 John 3:20). He knows the plans He has for us, to help us and free us to hope (Jeremiah 29:11). If we truly believe this, we must trust Him, knowing that He will work it all out for His glory and to our benefit; even when it doesn't feel like it at the time. The Lord has our best interests at heart, He is there beside us, never to forsake us (Hebrews 13:5). He will redeem what we think we've lost. He has and does comfort us so that we can comfort others (2 Corinthians 1:4).

We can think of our hurts and wounds as battle scars; scars that help us remember that pain is not forever, that we weathered the storm, and that God walked us through it all.

Father, help me to be a comfort to others
through their pain, as you have
comforted me through mine.

REFLECTION:
Do you know God's plans for you? Not just that they are good, but some of the specifics? We can ask Him to reveal His intentions and to be on board with Him.

Suggested Scripture Reading: Psalm 147; 2 Corinthians 1:3–4

THE BATTLE AHEAD

BARBARA WILLIS

We are human, but we don't wage war as humans do.

2 CORINTHIANS 10:3

The United Negro College Fund has a slogan: "A Mind Is A Terrible Thing To Waste." How many people know that the mind is never wasted? It is always active. The mind is at work even when we are asleep. Everything that has happened to us since birth is stored away in the mind, both good and bad. We can't get rid of it.

The mind is so powerful that it can actually lead our behavior. After all, "For as he thinketh in his heart, so is he" (Proverbs 23:7 KJV). It is at the center of our decisions for or against God's will. "I want to do what is good, but I don't. I don't want to do what is wrong, but I do it anyway" (Romans 7:19).

How can we be delivered from the evil, and adhere to good? We can intentionally discipline our minds to think about "what is true, and honourable, and right, and pure, and lovely, and admirable. Think about things that are excellent and worthy of praise" (Philippians 4:8).

That is a tall order: to resist storing up and keeping records of all the hurts, pain, resentments, and bitterness we experience over the years. The wrong decisions, the failures—all there warring with the mind—can cause damage to us, in our relationship with others, and in our relationship with God. God has told us when we keep records of wrongdoing active, we cannot love Him or others as we might. These

51

"strongholds" keep us from Christian living, and keep us in spiritual struggle, though we do not have to stay there:

> *"For though we live in the world, we do not wage war as the world does. The weapons we fight with are not the weapons of the world. On the contrary, they have divine power to demolish strongholds. We demolish arguments and every pretension that sets itself up against the knowledge of God, and we take captive every thought to make it obedient to Christ"* (2 CORINTHIANS 10:3–5 NIV).

As believers, we have divine power to live in an intentional way. We have full permission from God to ask Him to help obliterate those thoughts that weigh us down and keep us from living purposefully and joyously. We can trust that He will answer that sincere request according to His will (1 John 5:14). We will always, as Paul did, struggle with the war of our own flesh against the Spirit of God that is in us (Romans 7:24); and it will take commitment, new every day, to refute and lead away every one of those negative thoughts.

What is good? What is lovely? What is gracious? Let's commit together to employ the spiritual energy required to turn our minds toward those things, and toward trusting in our good God!

REFLECTION:
What is my focus in thought? In behavior?

Suggested Scripture Reading: Psalm 144:1–2;
2 Corinthians 10:3–5

A Nature Like Ours

Eric Moore

Elijah was a man with a nature like ours.
JAMES 5:17 NKJV

As a teenager, I disliked reading. My parents encouraged me to no avail. But one day my younger brother introduced me to superhero comic books. I was hooked. Read every comic book I could get my hands on. I loved these characters' supernatural abilities. (I knew these were nothing more than modern day fables.)

Sometimes we view the people of Scripture as superheroes. But they were human beings like us. Take the prophet Elijah. "Elijah was a man with a nature like ours" (James 5:17 NKJV). He could be bold and brave one minute, timid and scared the next. Yet God used him. By God's power, Elijah defeated four-hundred and fifty prophets of Baal on Mount Carmel (1 Kings 18:22–40). And then he ran when Queen Jezebel threatened his life (1 Kings 19:2). One wonders, *Shouldn't he have celebrated rather than run?* Well, Elijah was human.

Elijah may have had a lack of faith that God would protect him. He may have been discouraged that the nation was not turning to the Lord even after the defeat of the Baal prophets. Maybe he thought he was wasting his time serving the Lord; he was still a fugitive. However, the key is *where* he was running. Elijah headed to Mount Horeb, the mountain of God (1 Kings 19:7–8). The place where God had met Moses before him (Exodus 3).

Many of us have a special place where we meet God. It may be at the park or at the kitchen table. It is not only during the day-to-day devotion that we commune with Him but also during the difficult times of our journey when we need to run to Him.

> *Lord, thank You that You're not looking for superheroes and that You meet us when we need You, everyday, including those times when we need special encouragement and empowerment.*

REFLECTION:
The Lord is always near to those who seek Him.

Suggested Scripture Reading: Isaiah 38:1–6

Living Single

Linda Washington

But seek first the kingdom of God.
MATTHEW 6:33 NKJV

"I won't ever marry."

When I heard those words from a Campus Crusade leader during my junior year in college, I thought she was joking. All of my male friends who had heard her speak wanted to date her! Why on earth would she choose to be single when everyone seemed to want to be with her? All I wanted to do was find a boyfriend and eventually get married.

Flash forward several years to my twenty-eighth birthday. No one in my family had reached this age without being married. Yet I still waited for someone to "put a ring on it," as Beyoncé sang. Though I had had three serious relationships, all had ended in a breakup.

I pleaded with God Hannah-style (see 1 Samuel 1) to send the right man my way, believing I couldn't live a full life without a spouse. After all, God created marriage, as Genesis 2:18–24 reveals. It's not good for a person to be alone, right?

God answered my prayer in a way I hadn't expected. He gave me a profound contentment with being single. More than two decades have passed since that prayer. I'm still single.

A young man at my church recently asked me, "Why did you never marry?" I responded with 1 Corinthians 7. The apostle Paul, in writing to the church at Corinth, had some instructions for them about marriage and singleness. In verses 7–8, Paul wrote, "I wish that all of you were as I am. . . . It is good . . . to stay unmarried, as I do" (NIV). Later in the chapter, he added, "I would like you to be free from concern. An unmarried man is concerned about the Lord's affairs— how he can please the Lord" (7:32 NIV).

Paul is not preaching against marriage. He has plenty to say about marriage in the chapter. Instead, he reminds us that singleness, like marriage, is a gift. Yet singleness is not always celebrated as such. We're told to "keep praying for that spouse" rather than how to live as a single person. I've had some difficult conversations with well-meaning friends who equate being alone with being less than whole. But as a single person, you're not really alone. God is with you. In Him you are complete.

Singleness is not a gift for everyone. Paul acknowledged that in verse 7: "But each of you has your own gift from God; one has this gift, another has that." God chose for me to be single. And that's the whole point, isn't it?—God's right to choose for our lives.

Still, for many who are single today, the struggle is real. Maybe this is your struggle. God will grant contentment and purpose to all who ask and to those who choose to wait on Him. He wants you to seek His desires for your life (Matthew 6:33)—whether you marry or remain single.

REFLECTION:
Take time to pray, asking God for His plan for your life, whether you marry or remain single.

Suggested Scripture Reading: 1 Corinthians 7:7–9, 25–28, 32

Prelude

Shaquille Anthony

My suffering was good for me, for it taught me to pay attention to your decrees.

Psalm 119:71

In life, we face many difficulties that shake us. We may assume we're going through struggles as a result of what we've done, and that God is allowing a struggle because He's punishing us. It's easy for us to automatically assume that there was something done that then results in affliction and pain.

But I beg to differ and the reasoning is simple; there is purpose in everything in life. Everything, whether we view it as good or bad. Take the blind man in John 9, *intentionally* born that way. Everyone questioned Jesus about what the man had done that caused him to be born blind (v. 2). Jesus told them that the man had done nothing and people still questioned Jesus—even about the actions of the blind man's forefathers—but Jesus told them that no one had done anything, and that He had allowed for the blind man to be born that way so that the works of God would be displayed (v. 3). To everyone else, this seemed unreasonable, but God was setting the blind man up to be able to *witness*—that He is real and He is a healer.

The Bible goes on to declare that God spat on the ground and slapped the mud onto the blind man's eyes and told him to go wash in the Pool of Siloam (v. 6). After washing, the blind man instantly could see for the first time in his life (v. 7).

Now, the blind man who had been a beggar probably had thought previously that was his life, his end—begging. Maybe he had wondered why he had been born afflicted. After God healed him, he began to understand the significance of his affliction (v. 30).

Right now, any of us can face a situation or circumstance that puts us in an unsure space. But can we *see* that pain, affliction, and suffering can be purposeful? What if God chooses to display His power through an affliction we have to endure? What brings us pain can shed light on who He is and His power. Instead of thinking we are stuck, we can realize God can allow us to go through struggle *and bring us out*. When God brings us out, it's up to us to tell of His goodness and power.

But what the devil will try to do is hem you up and get you to keep your mouth closed. He doesn't want us to talk about what God has done for us. He doesn't want others to know that God is a healer, mind-regulator, heart-fixer, burden-bearer, restorer, and that He is peace that "surpasses all understanding" (Philippians 4:7 NKJV).

People need to hear your story and mine; our problems and issues—and how God brought us out. Our testimonies that reveal who He is—who Jesus is—can have a domino effect, drawing people to His power.

REFLECTION:
Could it be possible that your struggle or affliction can be purposeful? How might God work in your life? What is He revealing in and through you?

Suggested Scripture Reading: Psalm 119:1–24

Double Trouble

Juliet E. Cooper Allen

*Dear brothers and sisters, when troubles of any
kind come your way, consider it an opportunity
for great joy.*

JAMES 1:2

I sat in the exam with jolts of pain coursing through both
my arms. Waiting for the doctor to read my X-rays. I worried. *Could they both be broken?*

Less than two hours before, I had been at a church picnic,
playing volleyball. "I got it!" I had yelled, lunging forward.
With eyes trained on the ball, I was ready to volley it over the
net when I tripped and crashed. Landing hard, jarring pain
shot through my left and right arms. Hobbling to the park
shelter, I plunged my hands into the icy waters of a drink
cooler, to soothe the ache.

The knock on the door interrupted my anxious thoughts.
In walked the doctor, X-rays in hand. "Well, you managed
to fracture both wrists." I groaned. Throughout childhood
I had never broken a bone and now I had broken two at once.
Ouch! Double trouble!

Then, a prompting of the Holy Spirit came with the
admonition of James 1:2. *Joy? You have got to be kidding!*
Breaking both wrists was an unexpected, unwelcomed dis-
ruption to all my summer plans, including my twenty-fifth
high school reunion. Who would manage our home, care for
our children, prepare meals? *And what about my personal care?*
The immediate future looked bleak. I could see no reason for

joy. Yet, God was about to show me again that He can bring good out of bad situations.

You know, sometimes we take things for granted. When I was restricted from using my hands, I gained a new appreciation and gratitude for hands—my own hands that were on the mend and the helping hands of family members who served and assisted me.

When I had to be driven everywhere, I discovered how hard it was to relinquish my independence. While I was frustrated by my seven-week limitation, I realized that some people suffer lifelong disability. They depend on others for everything, always. Could this also be how senior adults feel in their sunset years as they become ever more dependent on others? In my trouble, God opened my eyes to the afflictions of others and heightened my compassion. He also sensitized me to opportunities for future ministry.

I never realized that my trouble, which caught me off guard, could activate gratitude, humility, patience, and compassion in my life. As we are reminded: "in all things God works for the good of those who love him, who have been called according to his purpose" (Romans 8:28 NIV). *All things?* I had wondered. What good could two broken wrists bring? Surprisingly, God did His work in the hidden places of my heart. And it *was* good. It was an opportunity for growth!

REFLECTION:
How do we react when we face a trial? Or lose some aspect of control over life, even due to others' behavior?

Suggested Scripture Reading: Genesis 50:15–22; James 1:2–4; James 5:14

Our Lord Lifts

Marva Washington

*When you lie down, you will not be afraid; when
you lie down, your sleep will be sweet.*

Proverbs 3:24 NIV

Whenever there was thunder or lightning, my younger
daughter would lie down on the sofa and go to sleep.
When it was over, no one had to awaken her; she seemed to
know the storm had passed.

When I was young, we all were made to get in the bed
with our mom when storms came, night or day, even when
it was stifling hot. "God was speaking" is what I understood
as the reasoning. And if the sun came out while it was still
raining, superstition taught us that the devil was "beating his
wife," whoever that unfortunate creature was supposed to be.
I was determined my daughters would never know how fearful I was of storms and going to sleep in the dark.

As adults, one night my sister decided to take my girls and
give me a break, enabling me to have some "me-time" while
my husband went away. Sadly, I had not yet taken hold of
God's promises: "When you lie down, you will not be afraid;
yes, you will lie down and your rest will be sweet" (Proverbs
3:24 NKJV). Or, "I will both lie down in peace, and sleep;
for You alone, O Lord make me dwell in safety" (Psalm 4:8
NKJV).

When I went to lie down in the quietness of my home,
I was fearful. I determined to take only a short nap—and with
all of the lights on. When I awakened, I saw that the sun was
shining and the clock read six o'clock. I had slept hard, lights

on, doors unlocked, windows open. And it was morning! God had comforted and protected me through the night. I could hardly contain my gladness. With my guard down and mind opened, God began teaching me lessons, even in in my sleep.

I made a promise to the Lord then, and to this day it's lights out when I go to bed. And in times when I become worried or fearful, I pray for others. I'm trusting the Lord, experiencing God's help, and the assurance that He can keep me and my family day and night. I'm letting God handle my fears.

REFLECTION:
What are you afraid of? Face it with God's Word, despite your fear, and watch Him work.

Suggested Scripture Reading: Psalm 3:1–6; Proverbs 3:24–26; 2 Timothy 1:7

Asking the Right Questions

Michael Lyles

He said to them, "It is not for you to know."
Acts 1:7 NIV

Why does my family have issues?
Why can't I find a good job?
Why are my friends so full of drama?
Why are my children acting crazy?
Why is it so hard to find a good mate?
Why is there so much hatred in the world? Why do the people doing wrong seem to get ahead of the people who are trying to do things right?

Do you have questions? So do I.

Just before Jesus was "taken up" into a cloud 40 days after God resurrected Him from the dead, He had a talk with His disciples, who, along with the entire nation of Israel, were tired of living under the difficulties of Roman rule. They wanted God to restore His kingdom on earth and get "the man" off their backs (see Acts 1:6). Jesus had already told them that He would be leaving soon (John 7:33). This was the disciples' one last opportunity to ask Jesus about when their problems would be solved on earth.

That reminds me of our requests for answers to the kinds of questions we raise. When I was younger I had my own questions. *Why were we on food stamps? Why did my mother nearly die from questionable health care? Why were we nearly homeless on two separate occasions? Why did certain neighborhood police collect money from the dope dealers every Friday?*

Jesus answered His disciples' question in a way that no one wants to hear; "It is not for you to know" (Acts 1:7). He said that some questions would not be quickly answered and would remain a mystery according to God's timing and will. His followers would have to live a faith life in the midst of uncertainty and lack of clear answers. However, they would have the certainty that they would not be alone in the uncertainty. For though they didn't get the answer that they sought, they would soon receive the Holy Spirit, who would answer the most important questions and needs in their lives. They did not ask for the Holy Spirit. They did not ask for power and intimacy with God. They were asking different questions, questions that were not really relevant to their new lives in Christ.

Sometimes we, like the disciples, get so distracted by this world that we focus more on the wrong issues. We do not ask the right questions. However, God always gives us the right answers, even if we are not asking the right questions.

REFLECTION:
Which questions are getting in the way of my experiencing the fullness of God in my life now?

Suggested Scripture Reading: Job 42:1–5; Acts 1:6–7

When Momma's Not Enough

Michael Lyles

*When my father and my mother forsake me,
then the LORD will take me up.*

Psalm 27:10 KJV

Many people have "parent issues." There are those of us who believe that a mother or father has let us down. There can be unresolved anger about being abandoned or abused emotionally, physically, or economically. Some people feel forgotten or ignored, which is an insult as painful as other forms of abuse. Sadly, since ancient biblical times, the record reveals that there *are* mothers and fathers who have forsaken their children.

Even under the best of parenting, there will be times when parents can carry us only so far in addressing a life situation. Momma simply may not be "enough" to help, even under the best circumstances. Because there comes a time when our mothers and fathers will leave us to walk through situations in life without them. They may not be able to offer support, even if they want to. They can also be so traumatized by their own problems that they are simply unavailable. There are parents who are too sick, tired, or emotionally spent, or too overwhelmed by poor parental role models from their own past. They may not be able to help with life situations that are foreign to them, such as going to college if their child is the first to do so. Parents may seemingly "forsake us" for many reasons that sometimes can reflect neglect, but at other times can be innocent shortcoming. However, *feeling* forsaken is real and can trigger loneliness, anxiety, and stress.

God knows that life will often place us in circumstances where we come to the end of our resources, even when considering our parents and what they provide for us. We must remember, "The Lord will take me up" (Psalm 27:10). These times of "lack" call attention to His resources, love, and commitment to us. These are times that can encourage us to develop an ever deeper relationship with our heavenly Parent. Parents, friends, spouses, mentors will all "leave" us in some areas of our lives, even if for brief periods of time. But God. He will never leave us to encounter anything in life alone (Psalm 23). Whoever we feel may have abandoned us, He will take us up.

REFLECTION:
Who am I looking to for support, more than looking to God?

Suggested Scripture Reading: Psalms 1; 23; 27

Beautiful, Powerful, Hard

Renee Bell

*"God will bless everyone who does not reject me
because of what I do."*

Luke 7:23 CEV

On the evening of September 30, 2007, I was reading *The
Red Sea Rules: 10 God-Given Strategies for Difficult Times*
by Robert J. Morgan. The first of the 10 rules says, "realize
that God means for you to be where you are." Just as He
led Israel "like a flock," using Moses and Aaron to help them
reach the Promised Land (Psalm 77:19–20). I ended my reading that night thinking it was both a beautiful and a powerful
statement.

It was. The very next day, at 9:30 in the morning, I received
word that God had called one of my sons home to be with
Him. At that moment I recalled those beautiful and powerful
words of the evening before. Only then, in the face of such
heartrending news, those words became a *hard* saying. That's
when I went back and read the last sentence on page six of
the book: "The same God who led you in will lead you out."
*How, God, could You mean for me to be here, and how will You
lead me out? How will I ever be able to bury my child?* I thought.

God's Word provided all the answers. Like John the Baptist in Luke 7, when he was jailed and wondered if Jesus was
actually the Messiah, my circumstances caused me to question God. I found that His answer for me remained the same
as His answer for John.

> *And he answered them, "Go and tell John what
> you have seen and heard: the blind receive their*

67

*sight, the lame walk, lepers are cleansed, and the
deaf hear, the dead are raised up, the poor have
good news preached to them"* (LUKE 7:22 ESV).

Reading this, I came to understand that when we are surrounded by adversity on all sides our minds should reflect
on what we have "seen and heard" about the Lord; what we
already know about Him. It causes us to repeat to ourselves
and report to others all the places where God delivered us.
It prompts our hearts to write a "scroll of remembrance"
(Malachi 3:16) that honors His Name, defends His will for
our lives, and compels us to not take offense at His decisions.

"Realize that God means for you to be where you are."
Whatever life circumstances may surround us, we can turn
to find and embrace God's words by faith and watch God
part the Red Seas in our life, so we will be able to walk into
our tomorrow without living our life defined by whatever crisis we may be in: regretful about the past, frustrated in the
present, and worried about the future. We will take that walk
knowing that we are standing because of God's grace, and
we'll walk that grace, unoffended by whatever decisions He
makes on our behalf.

REFLECTION:
Have you ever been "offended" by something God did? Did
the situation work itself out anyway? What did you learn? Try
writing a "scroll of remembrance" to set in stone your memory of how God has worked in your life.

Suggested Scripture Reading: Psalm 77:19–20; Luke 7:18–23

How to Uncover the Cover-Up

Victoria Saunders McAfee

Do not quench the Spirit.

1 Thessalonians 5:19 NIV

In an episode of a popular television series, a prominent businessman got himself mixed up in a messy situation, resulting in the death of a young woman. The detectives struggled to piece together what had happened. The rest of the television program traced the businessman's feeble attempts to cover his tracks.

The first time the Bible uses the word *cover* is in reference to the sin of Adam and Eve. They ate the "forbidden fruit," experienced shame, and then foolishly attempted to find a way to hide from God (Genesis 3:1–13). Sadly, like the businessman and the first couple in the Garden of Eden, people think that cover-up is better than honest confession. However, lying and deception are like rotten vegetables in the back corner of the refrigerator; if you don't clean them out, they're going to put out a pungent odor every time you open the door. God asked Adam and Eve questions to get them to admit to their sin of disobedience. He called to Adam, "Where are you?" (v. 9). He asked Eve, "What have you done?" (v. 13).

Many ask the question, with so many churches in the US, why is our society still in such bad shape? Particularly in predominantly African-American communities alone, there appears to be at least one church on every other block in many cities. Is it possible that cover-ups could be quenching the movement of God's Spirit?

The businessman at the end of the television program ended up getting shot and killed trying to continue to clean up and cover up his mess. All he had to do was put aside his pride, tell the truth to the authorities, and face his consequences. Instead, his cover-up cost him his life.

After God spoke with Adam and Eve concerning their sin and its consequences, He provided them with proper clothing. Once we come clean with Him, He then covers us with Jesus's righteousness. We no longer have to hide but can come boldly into His presence (Hebrews 4:16).

REFLECTION:
Is there something you are attempting to hide? Bring it out into the open, confess it, and rest in God's mercy and forgiveness.

Suggested Scripture Reading: Ezekiel 16:4–13

Preaching Victory

James Perkins

But how can we sing the songs of the LORD while in a pagan land?

Psalm 137:4

Psalm 137 was written during the period of the Israelites' Babylonian captivity. They had been taken from their homeland in Jerusalem and enslaved in a foreign, hostile, strange land. Their lament:

> By the rivers of Babylon, there we sat down, yea, we wept, when we remembered Zion. We hanged our harps upon the willows in the midst thereof. For there they that carried us away captive required of us a song; and they that wasted us required of us mirth, saying, Sing us one of the songs of Zion. How shall we sing the LORD's song in a strange land? (vv. 1–4 KJV).

Lament filled the broken hearts of our African ancestors after a brutal, dehumanizing trip across the Atlantic to strange lands. They had been high priests and priestesses, princes and princesses—humans reduced to mere chattel and sold across several continents and outskirts.

The slavers did their best to separate these "goods" from their tribe, dialects, and family relationships to prevent any bonding that might unify them, and generate rebellion. Slave masters also were not quickly inclined to evangelize slaves; they didn't want slaves in any way to share the same status as masters. Hearing the gospel also required time that could be economically productive for owners. Longstanding English tradition also held that those who became Christian could no longer be held as slaves. And there was the prevalent belief that Black people didn't have a soul, so it was futile to expose them to the gospel.

However, some slave owners eventually had a change of mind. Certain white preachers boasted about how "Christianizing" the slave made for a better slave. The Society for the Propagation of the Gospel in Foreign Parts, an agency of the Anglican Church, had sent missionaries to the Americas with the clear mission to Christianize slaves.

The legal issue of holding Christian slaves had been settled to the satisfaction of the slave owner, who had been assured that the slaves would not be taught anything that might be adverse to their status. Slaves who were exposed to the gospel did not hear anything from the white plantation preacher that would lead them to believe that God disapproved of their status as slave, or that His will for them was freedom.

Despite those efforts to convert slaves to that "brand" of Christianity, slaves did not show any significant response to the gospel until the revivals of the Great Awakening of the 1730s and 1740s. The preaching of the acclaimed George Whitefield, John Wesley, and others generated a new religious fervor that swept across Europe and America. It challenged traditionalism and the rigid structures of the Church, emphasizing personal salvation through Jesus Christ and freedom and equality in the Spirit.

Some slave owners even began to acknowledge the slaves' new position in Christ and allowed them to attend their church services with them. In some few instances, they were even permitted to serve as deacons—and occasionally to preach. This new fervor and emphasis on "freedom" in the Spirit began to spread among the slaves.

While they went to services sponsored for them by their masters and listened to the sermons set before them by their master's preacher, they did not necessarily agree with the perversion of the gospel they heard. They clearly understood the hypocritical religion of their masters was not *true* Christianity, and they rejected that "gospel" of obedience to masters.

Slaves had not come to their horrid condition and hearing some so-called "gospel" as a blank slate. While every attempt had been made to separate them, they retained their memories, beliefs, and worldview about an all-powerful, Supreme Creator God who was Father of all humankind.

Most of the slaves had come from the coastal countries of West Africa. To these Africans, all life was sacred and there was one God who was Creator-Father of us all. So the slave filtered whatever the plantation preacher preached through his own African belief system and experience. Some slaves attended the services sponsored by their masters, but they also made time to have their own meetings where they could express themselves freely, practice their African traditions, provide a corrective to the preaching they had received from the plantation preacher, and strengthen and encourage one another.

Religion was the central area for the creation and re-creation of their sense of community.

The slaves had been introduced to a perverted version of the gospel. They had been introduced to a racist-centered gospel that had at the very heart of it oppression and a perversion of God's will: that they be slaves. But, as theologian Howard Thurman stated in one of his many works, *Deep River*,

> "By some amazing but vastly creative spiritual insight, the slave undertook the redemption of a religion that the master had profaned in his midst. They dismissed the white interpretation of the gospel and grabbed the true Bible message."

Our ancestors saw God as all-powerful. They saw, in Jesus Christ and His suffering and resurrection, victory over suffering, wrong, and oppression. They saw in the Holy Spirit acceptance; as children of God they embraced freedom to be themselves and to express themselves. In the Moses story in Exodus, they saw God on the side of the oppressed and ultimate deliverance from oppression.

They saw themselves and their condition in the Bible message, and this is what their preachers preached to them. Prophetic preaching may be defined as that brand of preaching that focuses on the "justice" theme of the Bible. Principally through the Old Testament prophets, God warned the king, the political head of state, about His displeasure with oppression of the poor, the orphan, and the widow.

Micah declared, "What doth the Lord require of thee but to do justly, and to love mercy, and to walk humbly with thy God" (Micah 6:8 KJV).

Amos trumpeted, "But let judgment run down as waters, and righteousness as a mighty stream" (Amos 5:24 KJV).

Jesus stood in the tradition of the Old Testament prophets. In presenting His mission, He quoted Isaiah 61:1:

> *"The Spirit of the Lord is upon me, because he has anointed me to proclaim good news to the poor. He has sent me to proclaim freedom for the prisoners, and recovery of sight for the blind, to*

set the oppressed free, to proclaim the year of the Lord's favor" (LUKE 4:18–19 NIV).

By this definition, prophetic preaching in the slaves' private gatherings or "invisible institution" away from masters focused on the evil of slavery, the injustice of the inhumane treatment of the slaves, and God's will that slaves be free by any means necessary.

Author Charles V. Hamilton points out in *The Black Preacher in America* that "some black preachers, especially in the North, but in a few isolated places in Southern slave states, vehemently opposed slavery and exhorted their people to rise up against the system by force and violence if necessary." To be sure, this "resistance" preaching was not the only focus of the slave preacher's preaching. Some preached "pacification and acquiescence" to slavery circumstances. Some preached comfort and hope, painting great pictures of heaven and the joy hearers would experience when they ended up there. The slaves could shout and emote and have their spirits revived.

There is overwhelming evidence that the slaves preferred their own Black preachers to white preachers because church meetings were enjoyable and Black preaching frequently was masterful. The core content of the Christianity the slaves had forged focused on the evil and injustice of slavery, the humanity of the slaves as children of God, and God's will that the slaves be free. And though the slave owner did not want this message preached to his slaves, the slaves themselves rejected the message and the preacher who did not preach this message about freedom in some way as it was seen that the slave's duty was obedience to God above all else.

The Reverend Highland Garnett says in an 1843 message to the slaves,

> To such degradation (as slavery) it is sinful in the ex-
> treme for you to make voluntary submission. The di-
> vine commandments you are in duty bound to rev-
> erence and obey. If you do not obey them, you will
> surely meet with the displeasure of the Almighty.
> Therefore it is your solemn and imperative duty to
> use every means, both moral, intellectual, and phys-
> ical that promises success.

We can only tell that a few Black preachers, such as Nat Turner, had the courage and boldness to turn their preaching into outright revolt. It is certain that every Black movement before the Civil War that was connected with either the abolishment of slavery or the improvement of free Blacks had Black preachers involved. The involvement of preachers like Harriet Tubman and others saw the contradiction between their status and worth before God and their status in a so-called Christian nation. Tubman escaped slavery and risked her own life, making nineteen trips to the South to deliver hundreds of slaves.

Our ancestors chose to view their suffering through a lens of hope, believing their enduring hope would allow their children to have a better future. They saw that Jesus did not simply suffer for the sake of suffering. That God Himself authorized Jesus's suffering and authenticated His suffering in the Resurrection. Christ's suffering became liberating. And they believed in this liberation in the face of their own humiliation and struggle, envisioning this victory: that standing and speaking truth to power, no matter the consequences, then and now, creates victories now and for future generations.

REFLECTION:
What liberation might you gain from your struggle?

Suggested Scripture Reading: Isaiah 61

Obedience Brings Success

"Do not shout; do not even talk," Joshua com-
manded. "Not a single word from any of you until
I tell you to shout. Then shout!" (Joshua 6:10).

The walls of Jericho collapsed because the people obeyed
God's instructions. The people of Israel heard with their own
ears Joshua giving God's instructions, but it was their obedience in faith that brought them victory over their enemies.

> *When the people heard the sound of the rams'*
> *horns, they shouted as loud as they could. Suddenly,*
> *the walls of Jericho collapsed, and the Israelites*
> *charged straight into the town and captured it*
> (Joshua 6:20).

A *Bakongo* proverb says, *Zingu kia beto Bantu matu*, meaning,
"Our lifespan depends on our ears"—obedience brings suc-
cess. When we listen to and obey God, he will fight with us
(Joshua 1:8; 24:14–24).

—*Africa Study Bible* commentary on Joshua 6

PART TWO

JAN SPIVEY GILCHRIST

VICTORY

What Happens When People Pray . . . Together

Diane Proctor Reeder

There is a tearing of wings
by the clawing agents of the evil one

The night sky grows oppressively dark

In a small room, in a small house in the city
a battered remnant gathers . . .

Heads bowed, eyes closed
they beseech, cry, moan, bind, give thanks

After some delay,
the hands of the angelic host
scarred from combat
raise in victory

The attackers are vanquished
as the sacrifices of praise are given

The night sky is lit with the glory of God
While the garish sun looks on, jealous.

REFLECTION:

When you are in the throes of a struggle, close your eyes. Imagine angels interceding on your behalf. Imagine Jesus pleading your case before the Father as your Advocate. Then see how you feel.

Suggested Scripture Reading: Psalm 139:12; Ephesians 6:12

New Beginnings

Diane Proctor Reeder

It will be a jubilee year for you.

Leviticus 25:10

June 19 is a special day for African Americans to know their history. It is the holiday known as "Juneteenth." It is not an official national holiday, but one that is important because it's the designated time to remember and commemorate the day that African-American enslaved people received, at least by edict of the President of the United States, legal freedom from slavery.

Of course, we have yet to see the consummation of that edict, even in our time. Discrimination against African-Americans comes and goes in waves, often depending on who sits in our locally, state, and nationally elected offices, organizations, and for-profit companies. Yet, nevertheless, thousands if not millions of African Americans gather in places across the nation to celebrate that day.

That celebration of freedom is in the DNA of every human being. Jesus connects it so intimately to the truth: "And you will know the truth, and the truth will set you free" (John 8:32), almost as if freedom were the goal.

"Oh Freedom!"—the old spiritual bursts out with determination and resistance. Freedom is the principal thing in that rich, harmonious song and the singer insists that death itself is to be preferred to bondage.

The Scripture tells us, "don't get tied up again in slavery" (Galatians 5:1). We are not to have any master save God Himself.

Yet, we struggle. And in the struggling our bodies, minds, and hearts strain to this nebulous, undefined place called *freedom*. Isn't it ironic, then, that we already possess it? "So if the Son sets free, you are truly free," Jesus tells us (John 8:36); but we gloss over that verse, nodding in assent if we walk in chains of shame, and poverty, and frustration.

Here is an exercise for us: look up and compile every single Bible verse that includes the words *free* or *freedom*. Sit down in a chair, completely quiet. Read out loud every single one of those verses. Then decide what "freedom" really means. We will find ourselves rejoicing as did our enslaved ancestors on the day they found out that Abraham Lincoln "freed" them. But you and I will be truly free, inside and out . . . regardless of circumstances.

REFLECTION:
What does freedom really mean to me?

Suggested Scripture Reading: Leviticus 25

Singing into Battle

Patricia Raybon

*David replied to the Philistine, "You come to me
with sword, spear, and javelin, but I come to you
in the name of the LORD of Heaven's Armies—
the God of the armies of Israel, whom you have
defied."*

1 SAMUEL 17:45

I'm spending a Saturday morning on YouTube, listening to spiritual songs created by slave ancestors I'll never personally know. But I know their songs. Work songs. Praise songs. Solace songs. Healing songs. Singing these songs helped our forebears endure the worst of life—brutal capture, overwork, half-starvation, enforced poverty. Faced with this Goliath, they opened their mouths despite the pain and they sang. In cotton fields, rice paddies, sugarcane fields, brush arbors, and bayou backwaters; in blistering heat and bitter cold. Then to aid escape, they sang "signal songs"—"Wade in the Water," "Go Down, Moses," and other spirituals—to point themselves toward freedom.

Thus, they were like David, the singing shepherd boy. He defeated the Philistine Goliath—not with heavy armor or iron weapons, but first by opening his mouth. Declaring the glory of his conquering God, David said to Goliath: "You come to me with sword, spear, and javelin, but I come to you in the name of the LORD of Heaven's Armies—the God of the armies of Israel, whom you have defied" (1 Samuel 17:45).

Added David: "This is the LORD's battle and he will give you to us!" (v. 47).

I'm reminded of this while helping my husband, Dan, face multiple health challenges. His battle feels heavy some days because I struggle, as his wife, to stay ahead of my own work schedule while also going with him to doctor's appointments, picking up prescriptions, cooking meals, keeping house, and offering prayers and support. "Some days," I said to Dan recently, "it feels like we're fighting a giant Goliath."

As soon as I spoke, however, I thought of David—and of singing—and especially of a recent visit that Dan and I made to one of North America's greatest sites of singing, Fisk University. It wasn't a planned stop. We were visiting Nashville when relatives suggested we tour the Civil Rights Room at the downtown public library. While there we watched a film about young civil rights activists—Fisk students jailed for protesting, but who sang throughout the battle. Inspired by their courage, we made our way to Fisk and its Jubilee Hall. There we viewed a gorgeous mural of the original Fisk Jubilee Singers—who helped save their beloved school. How? They sang.

That, indeed, is what I'm doing this Saturday morning. Singing. Pretty loud, in fact. And so should you. When troubles come, don't pick up a heavy weapon. Just open your mouth. Then ignite God's power with praise.

REFLECTION:
What's your favorite spiritual or gospel song to sing? Take a few minutes now—and sing it!

Suggested Scripture Reading: 1 Samuel 17:41–47; 2 Chronicles 20:21–24

My Help!

ARTHUR JACKSON

*My help comes from the LORD, who made heaven
and earth.*

PSALM 121:2

For decades the renowned Brooklyn Tabernacle Choir has blessed multitudes through their soul-refreshing gospel songs. The award-winning choir includes voices from many cultures and life experiences, and their ministry has blessed millions around the world. One of their recordings is simply titled "My Help" and is based on Psalm 121. Taking their cues from passages like Psalm 121, God's people through the ages have identified the Lord as their source of "help" through their songs.

God's people are not strangers to singing about God's help. Our singing has been the primary medium for expressing our belief that the Lord is indeed our helper. The reformer Martin Luther got it right when he penned the words, "A mighty fortress is our God, a bulwark never failing; our helper He amid the flood of mortal ills prevailing." The truth of "A Mighty Fortress" resonates well with a people who have survived the ugly ravages of unfriendly forces in society. That's why other songs like Dr. Watts's "O God, Our Help in Ages Past" also touch our souls deeply: "Our God, our help in ages past, our Hope for years to come; our shelter from the stormy blast, and our eternal Home!"

And, we dare not forget another classic, which has made its way into the singing of our African-American past and present—"Father, I Stretch My Hands to Thee." Charles Wesley penned the great words, but African Americans have added the soulful sound. Many among us have joined in singing, "Father, I stretch my hands to Thee, no other help I know, if Thou withdraw thyself from me whither shall I go?"

Psalm 121 begins with a personal confession of faith in the One who brought all things into existence and the Creator God was the source of the psalmist's help (vv. 1–2). This meant several things for the biblical writer and it means the same for us. It means—stability (v. 3a); around-the-clock care (3b–4); 24/7 presence and protection (vv. 5–6); and preservation from all kinds of evil, for time and eternity (vv. 7–8).

Ponder the lyrics of Psalm 121. Do you feel alone, forsaken, picked on, abandoned, confused? Allow these words to refresh your soul with faith and courage. You're not alone; you don't have to do life or figure it all out on your own. Rather, rejoice in the earthly and eternal care of God that has been particularly demonstrated in the life, death, resurrection and ascension of the Lord Jesus Christ. And, whatever your next steps might be, take them with His help.

REFLECTION:
Where in your personal or family experience have you witnessed that the Maker of the universe is the helper of His people? What has been your response to Him?

Suggested Scripture Reading: Psalm 121

God's Surprise

Victoria Saunders McAfee

*Have mercy on me, O God, because of your
unfailing love. Because of your great compassion,
blot out the stain of my sins. Wash me clean from
my guilt. Purify me from my sin.*

PSALM 51:1–2

Bang! I jumped when the judge brought the gavel down
and pronounced "Divorced!" over my marriage. I felt like
a hammer shattered my already broken heart. A friend who'd
gone through a similar experience told me their judge ordered
six weeks of marital counseling before declaring *their* divorce
final. "Would You," I silently prayed, "give us the same kind
of judge? Could You intervene and save our marriage?" I hid
my mental mustard seed of faith in the corner of my spirit,
believing God for a miracle. Instead, the gavel hit the judge's
block, proclaiming *irreconcilable*; it's over!

I tossed my mustard seed of faith as I drove out of the
courthouse parking lot, angrily spitting verbal bullets out of
the car window. So much for not letting bitterness plant in
my heart; the root was deep, the bitter sprouts already fat and
branching out into a full-blown tree. I turned my back on
God for a season after this, choosing other ways to comfort
myself. I developed an unhealthy friendship with a coworker,
slept too much, ate lots of junk food, and even heard the
enemy of my soul whisper to me the idea of suicide.

Oh, *but God!* He had already walked over my wayward
path. He had His own set of plans to woo me back. So many
friends and family members fervently prayed. I had several

87

godly counselors. And my three children's sad eyes constantly cried out, *Mama, please get it together.* God reminded me of what I knew from the Bible, so I could realize, *if I keep walking in this direction, things are not going to end well.*

One thing God did during that time surprised me, and I still smile when I think back on it. He caused me to *long* for Him. I genuinely *missed* my part in my relationship with the Lord. I'd been used to talking to Him first thing in the morning and before I dozed off to sleep at night. When I needed wisdom, I was used to calling on Him. It got very hilarious at times. I'd be in mid-sentence praying about something . . . then I'd think, *Oh, I forgot, God, I'm not talking to You.*

What a joy to finally hit rock bottom and realize my stupidity. I took a long, tearful bath in Psalm 51. Thank you, King David, for penning such a beautiful prayer of confession and repentance. The first part of the prayer focuses on the wrong done, but in the second half David pleads for his relationship to be restored. He wanted that fellowship he had with the Lord before his adultery with Bathsheba and the murder of her husband (2 Samuel 11). He yearned to be close to the Lord once again.

What a *kind* God we serve. He answered David's prayer—and mine. He can create in us a brand new, spanking-clean heart and totally change our corrupt thinking (Psalm 51:10). The Lord restores our fellowship and our joy. None of us deserve God's grace because of our sin, but our heavenly Father delights in pouring grace out in this season.

REFLECTION:
Lord, thank You for Your cleansing power.

Suggested Scripture Reading: Psalm 51:1–14; Hebrews 12:14–16

All the Single Ladies (and Single Men)

Pamela Hudson

*When the devil had finished tempting Jesus, he
left him until the next opportunity came.*

LUKE 4:13

"Where are my happy, content, and confident singles?" is the
usual question at the beginning of my lectures on being
a Christian "single saint." I find that many Christian singles
are frustrated and puzzled about how to live their lives victo-
riously—and I sometimes count myself among that number!

There are three aspects of life that keep many of us distracted, disconnected, and derailed: the world (John 15:18),
the flesh (Romans 7:22–23), and the devil (1 Peter 5:8). Let's
take a look at Satan's devices for a minute. In Luke 4, God's
Spirit led Jesus to the desert where Satan would tempt Jesus
in the most critical areas:

PHYSICAL DESIRE (hunger): "If you are the Son of God, tell
this stone to become bread"(v. 3 NIV);

DESIRE FOR PERSONAL SAFETY (preservation of life): "If you
are the Son of God," he said, "throw yourself down from here
[from the Temple]" (v. 9); and,

DESIRE FOR SPIRITUAL AUTONOMY OR INDEPENDENCE: "If you
worship me, it will all be yours" (v. 7 NIV). The devil lied to
suggest he could give Jesus what He already owned: all the
kingdoms of the world, if Jesus would only worship him.

If the devil would do that to Jesus, it's not hard to imagine the strategies he would use to attack us!

How do we resist Satan's devices (something I know from experience is not easy)? Luke 4 gives us the blueprint. Jesus overcame the most intense temptations with the skillful use of God's Word. He followed the Holy Spirit's leading (Luke 4:1) and had a powerful listening session in the wilderness, where He fasted and prayed for 40 days. He paved a righteous path for us to follow.

And so, I urge us to be ready to move with the Holy Spirit for every step of our life journey. To recognize that power belongs to God alone. We can trust His sovereignty over our lives. Let's stay, as the older saints like to say, "prayed up." And anchor ourselves in the Word of God to experience victory. Let's be consistent and persistent to seek God and communicate with Him.

Jesus is the Lover of our souls. He can hold your life.

REFLECTION:

Is your frustration with being single interfering with your walk with God? How? What does Jesus's wilderness experience teach us about how to overcome that frustration?

Suggested Scripture Reading: Luke 4

My Declaration of *In*-Dependence

DIANE PROCTOR REEDER

All Scripture is God-breathed and is useful for teaching, rebuking, correcting and training in righteousness.

2 TIMOTHY 3:16 NIV

Have you ever taken a look at different church and denominations' doctrinal statements? It can be an interesting exercise. I admit, most are fairly standard and say much of the same. Of course denominations were formed precisely because individuals in the church disagree on key points— points, they would say, of this thing called "doctrine"—the collection of beliefs, teachings, and principles that make up the Christian faith.

But why is this reflection smack dab on the heels of a whole group of devotionals on *struggle*? Because what we focus on as "doctrine" defines how we think. And how we think about a thing determines how we feel, how we respond, and most importantly how we act . . . particularly related to our most pressing life challenges. In other words, our doctrinal understanding can determine the level of our victory.

If you think, as some preachers say as they quote David, "I am a worm" (Psalm 22:6), then you will act accordingly. But did God really intend for that plaintive cry of a guilt-ridden man to be elevated to the level of doctrine? I think not.

Let me suggest something different. Make up your own statement about your personal faith.

Well, not really just "make it up." Look through the Scriptures—read through the entire Bible in a year—and let the Holy Spirit underline the verses that resonate with your spirit. Use those verses to guide how you think for one entire year. Think of it as your own personal "Declaration of In-Dependence." You are after all living *in* dependence . . . on God. Do that, and you will be surprised at how differently you react to struggle.

Let me share with you my own declaration:

- I believe that I live in dependence on God every day.
- I believe that my body is a temple, that because of this every step I take is on holy ground. I must remember that every day.
- I believe that I have been set free by the Son of God to do the work of God according to the Word of God.
- I believe that I am both drawn to and blessed by God's mystery.

Consider doing this every year. Document each "Declaration." And notice how your *In*-Dependence changes over time. How it grows and blossoms into rich wisdom, based on your time in God's Word.

I stand before you, and God, a grateful woman today. Grateful because in the struggle, God is still speaking.

Let Him speak to you.

REFLECTION:
What are the parts of the Bible that speak to you right now? Can you write your own "Declaration" about them?

Suggested Scripture Reading: Psalm 139:13–18

What's Your Strategic Plan?

Henry Allen

*Those who are wise will shine as bright as the sky,
and those who lead many to righteousness will
shine like the stars forever.*

Daniel 12:3

What do you want to be when you grow up?" As a child,
you probably were asked that question a lot. Usually,
we don't know the answer, either because we don't know what
the range of options are, or because we don't have people we
can look to as examples. Then, we get out into the world as
young adults, and life's storms hit. What to do? How do we
move forward? Prayer.

Long ago, a man lived in a multiethnic, complicated society that was a world empire called Babylon. In its era, Babylon
was far greater than the United States in terms of the amount
of land and number of people that fell under its authority. As
a youth, this man was taken captive by a ruthless king from a
hostile society, away from family, loved ones, and all that was
familiar. That man was Daniel.

How did he survive all these traumas?

Daniel had a strategic plan for his life: no matter what,
he would always be devoted to God in *prayer*. In his youth,
Daniel overcame peer pressure and did not embrace ungodly
behaviors. He had teachers that gave him favor, even though
they did not understand his deep love for God. However, his
teachers and foes recognized his integrity and excellence—
for Daniel was always aware that God was watching him.
Later on, as a man, Daniel faced many crises as a prominent

government official, yet he never wavered in his devotion to God or in his prayer life. As a very busy university or college professor across four decades, Daniel's example has been a vital template for my life!

Because Daniel displayed such wisdom in his commitment and plan, he was able to shine. We, too, can live a life devoted to God and prayer no matter what pressures or storms we face in our families, on our jobs, and in our communities if we follow Daniel's example. Shine in God's wisdom like the stars and enjoy the journey of leading many to righteousness in Jesus Christ and for His eternal kingdom!

REFLECTION:
Do you have a strategic plan? What are the commitments you have made to yourself? To others? To God?

Suggested Scripture Reading: Daniel 1:8–15

WHO'S IN THE ROOM?

VICTORIA SAUNDERS MCAFEE

But when the Father sends the Advocate as my representative—that is, the Holy Spirit—he will teach you everything and will remind you of everything I have told you.

JOHN 14:26

After reading a passage about the Holy Spirit in a Bible-study group, one of the participants looked confused. "I grew up in a church that talked a lot about God and Jesus but taught very little about the Holy Spirit," she said. "Sadly, as a child, I was afraid of the Holy Spirit. The only time I heard the Spirit consistently mentioned was when someone was jumping around the church in an emotional frenzy, shouting, 'Halleluiah, thank You, Jesus.' I asked my parents and they said, 'she or he's got the Holy Ghost.' I'm sorry, all that looked scary to me and I wanted no part of any ghost, holy or otherwise."

There is a lot of misunderstanding about this third person of the triune God or Trinity. Yes, the Holy Spirit can bring about emotion. I must admit I have more head knowledge about the theology of God's Spirit than actual personal experience. At one point in my studies I picked up an "I-need-to-do-better" frame of mind. I placed too much weight of my Christian growth and maturity on my back. I battled with thoughts like, "I need to make wiser choices. I need to know my spiritual gift and I'd better use it to its full potential." There were always some kind of ten-step practices, procedures, and formulas in the materials I read.

On the other hand, when I take a real close look at the life and ministry of Jesus, I don't see striving or any hint of *self*-effort. Very few if any "one, two, three" methodologies. Instead, I see a total dependence on the Holy Spirit to fulfill His ministry here on earth, from the time His ministry started. After Jesus was led by the Spirit into the desert to be tempted (Matthew 4:1), "Jesus returned to Galilee, filled with the Holy Spirit's power. Reports about him spread quickly through the whole region" (Luke 4:14).

Jesus's final teachings to His disciples flow with references and instructions pertaining to the activity of the Holy Spirit. He was not only letting the disciples know who would take center stage after His resurrection, but he explained to them— "This is how; this is who empowered me to do God's will."

As I learn, I try my best to communicate to the women in my Bible study that the Holy Spirit is with us—"present in the room right now." He's ready and willing to teach us all things and guide us daily, moment by moment, second by second. Depending on the Holy Spirit is the difference between peace and frustration.

I've learned to ask the Holy Spirit to visit my "back rooms"; inspect my secret thoughts and impure motives. Many times, the Spirit has opened my eyes to issues hidden beneath my surface thinking. I'm beginning to see my life transformed in places where faithlessness and frustration resided.

REFLECTION:
The question is on the table: do we want a smooth, carefree, "trouble-free" life? Or do we want a life in which we can constantly testify about the power of God working in our lives?

Suggested Scripture Reading: John 14:15–21

Finding Contentment

Cheri Perron

*I have learned how to be content with whatever
I have.*

PHILIPPIANS 4:11

Wouldn't it be great to live a stress-free life? Wouldn't it be nice if we just had to go through one trial instead of struggling with life challenges for as long as life is in us? I would love that.

As I have struggled with chronic illness, I had come to the point where I accepted my condition. I depended on the Lord simply to "get me through" each day. After a long period of asking *why me*, the Lord had to show me, time and time again, that He is in control. When I finally embraced that, I surrendered my health to the Lord. I believed I had learned my lesson of contentment.

It became a much different situation when my child became ill. Not many stressors in life will cause greater anxiety than the illness of a child. All my greatest fears came roaring back. I couldn't understand. I was trusting the Lord with my life. Why couldn't I do this with the life of my child, who belongs to God? I *knew* that God is the one in control. My *heart* was a different matter.

Where was my faith? What happened to my focus? Here I was in a situation I had no control over, and I don't like feeling helpless. I couldn't pray because I didn't know what to say.

All I could say were three words: *Lord, fix it!*

Then I waited. I waited to hear God's voice say it would be all right. Deafening silence. I couldn't sit still. I was "walking anxiety." There was nothing I could do.

"Lord, afflict me instead!" I would pray. "Anyone but my child!" All of it was out of my control.

Of course, God needed my help.

Of course, He didn't.

I had failed in one of the most important lessons we can learn in life: how to relinquish control. In my attempt to control my son's illness, I took my focus off of God. All I could see was my situation. My son had my undivided attention; God, sadly, did not. But isn't that how we humans often behave in our attempts to control the circumstances of life?

Our strength and contentment must come from the Lord and the Lord alone. We become content and stronger in our faith when we spend time sitting at His feet, in His Word, allowing Him to speak to us. We have to trust and rely on Him, our source of strength. And when we do that we will trust the sovereignty of His will for us. Contentment is that condition of the heart that trusts in Him.

Lord, teach me how to keep my eyes focused on
You and not on simply what I see before me.

REFLECTION:
What is the condition of my *heart*?

Suggested Scripture Reading: Proverbs 19:23;
Philippians 4:11–13

Capturing the Caleb Spirit

Victoria Saunders McAfee

But because my servant Caleb has a different spirit and follows me wholeheartedly, I will bring him into the land he went to, and his descendants will inherit it.

Numbers 14:24 NIV

I want to finish my master's degree and go on to get a doctorate. I can hear the thunder of encouragement: *You go girl! That's what I'm talking about! Yeah, you can do it!* Did I mention I'm 62 years old now? "Oh." The cheerleading team just got severely cut. The inspirational chants died down to a whisper.

When I mentioned this desire to one friend he had the nerve to start talking to me about dementia, senility, and Alzheimer's. I angrily replied, "Did God tell you I was about to get any of those issues?"

He was relentless. "Well you know, at a certain age we have to be realistic that some of the things we wanted to do at 20 or 30 are not going to happen."

"I do agree, somewhat," I responded, determined to argue my point. "But I think some of us give up too soon. We blame physical ailments, family problems, and a host of other things to resign ourselves to sit on the couch and watch TV, giving in to discouragement."

Caleb, the biblical character, stands out as a senior whose attitude I really like. He and his buddy Joshua traveled with the multitude from Egypt, where they were appointed by Moses with ten others to go in and spy out the Promised Land. They, too, saw the giants and the many other obstacles facing the congregation, but their eyes were fixed on God. They believed His word over the obvious circumstances. Because of their faith God allowed them to enter the land, but the rest of the multitude died in the wilderness. These two men refused to give up in their senior years in spite of all the challenges they faced throughout their lifetime. In fact, Caleb told everyone, "I'm strong as I was 40 years ago" (Joshua 14:11 paraphrase).

Why is it that some seniors are sitting around drowning themselves in regret and sorrow while others are climbing mountains, winning athletic competitions, and accomplishing educational degrees?

Is it in the quality of their "cheerleaders" (or lack thereof)? Or are there distinctive, intrinsic qualities that determine how long a person stays active and vital, embracing high expectations and assuming the best?

Be careful who you listen to. We need to turn a deaf ear to people who are negative and discouraging. Offer a deaf ear to people who discourage. Caleb listened to God's promises and tuned out the negativity all around him.

I'll be walking across that stage getting my doctorate before my 70th birthday, if God says the same. And His voice is the one that truly counts.

REFLECTION:
Got any dreams you've put on the shelf? Maybe today is a good day to take them down and pray about them again.

Suggested Scripture Reading: Numbers 14:5–9; Joshua 14:10–12

Into the Deep

Georgia A. Hill

*John baptized with water, but in just a few days
you will be baptized with the Holy Spirit.*

Acts 1:5

I used to be scared of deep water. I almost drowned, or at
least that's how it seemed in my eleven-year-old mind.
I was right at the edge of the pool and started to bob and gasp
for air. It seemed like forever until the lifeguard extended that
metal hook to me. No more deep water for me after that. Of
course I had lots of company on the sidelines.

Turns out that Christians are called to "deep water."
Something happens when we are submerged in Christ's life:
a cleansing, a renewing, a resurrection. It is through this bap-
tism that we die to the old and rise to new life in Christ. We
must be baptized in the Spirit, submerged completely and
utterly. No more touching the bottom, far away from the
sides and the shore, carried by the current of God to whom-
ever or wherever God decides.

A camp counselor took me out of the kiddie pool, telling
me I was too big to be with the little ones, and taught me how
to swim in a manmade lake with sloping sides and a depth of
20 feet. She was an excellent counselor. Eventually I became
a junior lifeguard! In order to pass the test we had to rescue
a person struggling in deep water. "Whatever you do," the
instructor bellowed, "Don't stay on the surface of the water as
you approach the drowning person!" We were told that one
cannot save a drowning person by remaining on the surface.
When a drowning person sees the rescue swimmer, they will

try to lift their body up by pushing the rescuer's head under the water. If the rescuer stays on the surface, the drowning person will drown the rescuer. We were taught to dive deep just as we approached the drowning person and swim around so we could grab them from the back and swim them back to shore.

Perhaps it is time for more of us to go deeper with the Holy Spirit. People don't need platitudes; they need power! Jesus said, "But you will receive power when the Holy Spirit comes upon you. And you will be my witnesses, telling people about me everywhere—in Jerusalem, throughout Judea, in Samaria, and to the ends of the earth" (Acts 1:8). So many are drowning—in sin, hopelessness, desperation, and fear—but "surface-swimmers" cannot save them. Spiritless swimmers may find themselves pushed under the water by those who need rescue. But those who have been baptized in Christ's Holy Spirit have power to witness to those in deep trouble, those who need the saving love of Jesus. Come on, let's go into the deep.

REFLECTION:
What might be keeping you in the "shallows"?

Suggested Scripture Reading: Psalm 42:7; Acts 1:1–8; Romans 6:4

"I Ain't No Junk!"

YULISE WATERS

Thank you for making me so wonderfully complex!

PSALM 139:14

Have you ever had a day when you felt less than special? (And that's putting it nicely.) You just felt like you weren't "getting it right." Not smart enough. Quick enough. Articulate enough. Tall enough, thin enough, pretty enough, handsome enough, strong enough, organized enough. And everything you did or said seemed to be, or at least felt like, the wrong thing to say or do. Such moments are not uniquely yours. We have all had some variation of those experiences.

David is one who understood the shift in perspective that comes with looking to the Lord. In these words, he magnifies God's awesomeness by acknowledging the wonder of His creation—David himself. Every time I read Psalm 139, "I feel my Help coming on!" as we say in the Black church tradition.

When the press and pressures of life have us feeling less than successful, less than powerful, less than smart, less than confident, less than special, less than creative, less than _____ (you fill in the blank), remember that God Almighty took the time to knit us together specifically the way we are. When society tries to discount, dismiss, deny, and misidentify our unique characteristics whether they be personality, perspective, appearance, passion, interests—whatever—remember that God took the time to make "all the delicate, inner parts of [your] body" (Psalm 139:13). And God don't make no junk! You have a right to stand tall, bold, and confident because the Creator of heaven and earth and of the entire universe—what we see and what we don't see, what we know about and what we don't even know to think about—took the time to specifically craft you just the way you are and He has a plan for your life.

> *Lord, when we feel down and out and flat out*
> *defeated, help us to remember that we have*
> *been fearfully and wonderfully made by Your*
> *hand. Help us to catch a glimpse of what*
> *You see when you see us. Let us embrace the*
> *beauty and greatness of ourselves, thereby*
> *giving glory to Your name for Your*
> *marvelous works. In Jesus's name.*
> *Amen.*

REFLECTION:
Think about God's purposes in some aspect of your physical attributes or personality.

Suggested Scripture Reading: Psalm 139:13–16

SPIRITUAL TRAINING

KENNETH PERRON

Do not waste time arguing over godless ideas and old wives' tales. Instead, train yourself to be godly.

1 TIMOTHY 4:7

Growing up in Texas, sports played a big part in my life. I can honestly say that sports kept me in school and on the right side of the law. I had good parents and coaches guiding and training me. They helped me understand that without good training and discipline, I couldn't succeed in sports at a higher level, much less succeed in life.

I developed a training regimen: practice in the morning before school, practice after school, do my homework, sleep, and start that all over the next day. For years this was my daily routine. I was focused and disciplined in my training.

There were times when my father or others would tell me how they used to train "back in the day," just as I would later tell my son how I trained "back in my day." Sadly, some of those "back in the day" methods were incorrect or proven less valuable than originally thought. There was no real understanding behind them. Some ideas and methods were, in fact, myths—and in this case, old *men's* tales.

When it comes to living a godly life, Paul tells us, "Have nothing to do to with godless myths and old wives' tales," (1 Timothy 4:7 NIV). I'm not saying don't listen to others. But we must understand, from a spiritual perspective, that godless myths are plain old lies from the devil and serve no purpose for us. As for old tales, they are for the most part passed down from generation to generation and more for the sake of tradition than accuracy.

Paul ends by saying "rather" or "instead of" tales and godless myths, "train yourself to be godly." How do you train yourself to be godly? It's no secret that God has already given us everything we need to live a godly life, but it's up to us to put everything into practice. God places His power in us at salvation in order to live a godly life. We see that "In his great mercy he has given us new birth into a living hope through the resurrection of Jesus Christ from the dead" (1 Peter 1:3 NIV).

His hope allows us to shed the things that weigh us down. You must "throw off everything that hinders and the sin that so easily entangles" you (Hebrews 12:1 NIV). God allows us to get rid of every association, habit, and tendency that hinders godliness. At the same time, we can develop spiritual discipline, the consistent exercising of self-control and development of habits that produce godly character and patterns of behavior. Engaging in spiritual training through connecting with knowledgeable Christians allows them to mentor us. Faithfully attending a church provides us not only with worship opportunities but also teaches us God's Word, and spiritual obedience, as we submit our will to God's will, His Word, and His way.

Ask God today what you need to give up, and what you need to put on, in order to live a godly life.

Lord, I thank You for coming into my life and giving me all I need to live a godly life.

REFLECTION:
Is there anything hindering you from living a godly life?

Suggested Scripture Reading: 1 Corinthians 9:24–27

LISTEN!

GEORGIA A. HILL

For we walk by faith, not by sight.
2 CORINTHIANS 5:7 NASB

Pitch black! That's all I could see when I walked out—on stage. We had practiced our liturgical dance on that stage for two days, but during rehearsal the house lights were on. The seats and the aisles of the theatre became a sort of visual anchor for me. No one told me that on the night of the program I would not be able to see anything or anyone in front of my face! I was so disoriented that initially I lost my footing. I stumbled for the first few beats of the music.

Life can be that way sometimes. Out of nowhere, we find ourselves in an unrehearsed moment. Sudden calamity strikes and we lose our footing. Death, destruction, disease, or other dread that comes upon us without warning can cause us to stumble because suddenly the landscape changes; things no longer look familiar. Of course, our eyes can play tricks on us. What looks like a peaceful family dinner can suddenly erupt into WWII. What appears to be a perfectly reasonable relationship can turn into conflict, violence, or abuse. Is it wise to rely solely on what we see with our eyes? The Bible teaches us that we should live by faith and not by sight (2 Corinthians 5:7). We walk because we trust God! We step forward, not because we can see which way we are going, but because the hand of God is leading us and we trust His hand.

The walk of faith is a *listening* walk. We faith-walk when we listen more than we look. I stumbled that night in the theatre until I remembered to *listen*. The music called me back to the right steps. As I listened I got back into the rhythm and the movement of the dance.

Our faith is sound-dependent too. "So faith comes from hearing, and hearing by the word of Christ" (Romans 10:17 NASB). Our faith grows as we listen to the Word of God. The more we allow the Word of God to be our "music," we will not stumble in sudden darkness; we will dance. God's voice will lead us into His light, into the rhythm and dance of life in Him.

REFLECTION:
Close your eyes and listen; God is speaking.

Suggested Scripture Reading: 1 Kings 19:11–12; Psalm 23:1–3; John 4:24–26

Let's Celebrate Unsung Heroes!

Henry Allen

Now there was a believer in Damascus named Ananias. The Lord spoke to him in a vision, calling, "Ananias!"
"Yes, Lord!" he replied.

ACTS 9:10

I have always admired "unsung heroes" in the church and the ministry. They are often overlooked for their labors, efforts, and achievements. Some unsung heroes serve in a church's hospitality ministry, cleaning up messes after the church picnic. Some teach in children's church, facing obstacles without rewards. Others give silently and steadfastly, making it possible for others to thrive or flourish. Many do the "dirty work" of ministry or evangelism without fanfare or title. Like those who serve faithfully inside the church Sunday after Sunday— as well as those who serve outside the church—many saints of God are unsung heroes.

Yet the Lord knows who you are and where you serve Him obediently. In the verse above, we find that Ananias was an unsung hero as he obeyed the Lord's instruction despite the real possibility of acute danger to himself, his family, and the church in Damascus. In anointing and baptizing the terrorist Saul of Tarsus, who would later become the apostle Paul (the Lord's prime missionary to the non-Jewish world), Ananias was unsung. We do not know much about him. But, without Ananias and his undeniable faithfulness to the Lord, there may never have been the apostle Paul as we know him today across generations.

Why was Ananias able to become an unsung hero to Christ's church in a turbulent era? First, when called, he *surrendered* to the Lord with unquestioned *obedience*. Potential risks and danger did not deter his devotion to the Lord Jesus Christ! Secondly, Ananias possessed unshakable *faith*. He knew the Risen Christ has all power in His hands, having achieved supreme victory through His resurrection from the dead! Lastly, Ananias *trusted* in the Lord's instructions, enabling him to witness the unsurpassable impact of Paul's ministry to the world. All in all, I think Ananias was delighted to observe the unfolding of the Lord's great plan.

Perhaps, you too, are an unsung hero in your church, family, community, workplace, and ministry. Hold on! Persist in your faithful obedience and watch the Lord do great things as a result of your unsung heroism!

Let us always celebrate our unsung heroes; they are indispensable allies to the building of God's kingdom!

REFLECTION:
Do you know any unsung heroes in your church or community? Are you one?

Suggested Scripture Reading: Hebrews 11:32–39

Legacy of Faithfulness

Arthur Jackson

Moses was faithful as a servant in all God's house. . . . But Christ is faithful as the Son over God's house.

HEBREWS 3:5–6 NIV

Perched on the upright piano in the church where I became a Christian rests the same bell that years ago rang out to notify us that Sunday school was about to end. While the bell has endured the test of time, the person who controlled the bell each week has been in heaven for years. But, like the bell, his legacy endures.

If there ever was a faithful man, it was Brother Leoper Justice. Faithful husband to his wife, Pattie; a faithful worker at his postal service job; and each Sunday he was present at his post as Sunday school superintendent. Perhaps you know a faithful man or woman cut from the same cloth.

Hebrews 3:5–6 brings two faithful men into focus. Moses was a faithful "servant"; Jesus was a faithful "Son." Moses was a "one-of-a-kind" leader for God's people (Numbers 12). More significantly, Jesus is God's Son from eternity (Hebrews 1). What the two had in common was faithfulness to their appointed mission; that is faithfulness we can share with them.

Your role or assignment in the Christian family is not insignificant nor does it go unnoticed by the One with whom it really matters. You, too, are leaving a legacy. May it be one of faithfulness.

REFLECTION:

Father, Help me to leave a legacy of faithfulness after the example of the Lord Jesus and after the examples of faithful men and women who have served before us. Amen.

Suggested Scripture Reading: Hebrews 3:1–6

How Can You Mend a Broken Heart?

Georgia A. Hill

*The Spirit of the Sovereign LORD is upon me, for
the LORD has anointed me to bring good news
to the poor. He has sent me to comfort the brokenhearted and to proclaim that captives will be
released and prisoners will be freed.*

ISAIAH 61:1

I can still hear the question; a song and a cry by the soulful
singer: "How can you mend a broken heart?" It is a song
from our rhythm and blues past. The world offers melodies,
self-help and psychiatric help, pills and mind power, spa trips
and head trips, coping skills and fitness skills but is there
really ever healing? Truly, how can a heart broken by betrayal,
abuse, neglect, or violence ever be mended? Even though we
shake our heads, wring our hands, offer tissue and pepper-
mints, and utter a quick prayer, is this bringing *healing*?

We say that Jesus heals, but the healing that He offers will
take more than *words* of faith. It will require an *act* of faith:
actually giving one's heart to the Lord. No one gets well by
talking *about* the doctor. We have to actually *go to* the doctor.
I have been more than once; to Doctor Jesus, that is.

When I graduated from college my spirit and my heart
were broken. I was disconnected from my faith and had
stopped going to church. Later, two dear friends, church girls,
saw my sickness and took me to the only real hospital they
knew. Back in church, I learned slowly and gradually to give
my mind and my emotions, my thoughts and my desires into
the hands of Jesus Christ and to allow Him to do the fixing

and the mending. It was like being in the operating room when my father, who is a surgeon, stitched up my wrist after I cut it on a mirror. He first took away the pain with topical anesthetic, then he thoroughly washed the wound, making sure all pieces of broken glass were removed, and then he carefully stitched me up and wrapped gauze around the area. It was not me who did the surgery, but my father. It was not me who fixed it, but he.

God sent Jesus to bind up the brokenhearted (Isaiah 61:1). He has been sent to wrap our wounds tightly in His love. If we will give our whole heart to Jesus He will heal us and give us new life. But we have to allow Him to do the new thing in us (Isaiah 43:19). When Daddy removed the bandage on my wrist, he told me that over time my scar would fade. By this time, more than 40 years later, it is barely perceptible; a reminder of the gift of mending on earth but a testimony to the mending that comes from heaven.

Thank You, Jesus for taking away the pain,
for washing away my sins, for stitching up my
wounds, for wrapping me in Your love, and for
being the Healer of my broken heart. Thank
You for being the Doctor who is always on call.

REFLECTION:
What other comparisons can you make between Jesus and a medical doctor? What do these comparisons say to you about how Jesus heals?

Suggested Scripture Reading: Isaiah 40; Isaiah 61:1–3; Jeremiah 29:10–11

Door of Hope

Juliet E. Cooper Allen

But after a while, the brook dried up.

1 Kings 17:7

What do you do at wit's end? When you hit a brick wall of problems with few options in sight? When you come to the end of your rope and the end of your money?

In that desperate place, God sees our distress.

In 1 Kings 17, we read the story of Elijah. After announcing an upcoming drought to King Ahab, God sent Elijah to the Kerith Ravine. Ravens brought him food and he drank from nearby Brook Cherith. After a while, the brook dried up. How would he survive? At his point of need, God shows up and provides a door of hope. He sends Elijah to a widow in Zarephath.

In the summer of 1997, our family needed a door of hope when we faced a serious financial drought. Talk about a desperate time! My husband was transitioning to a new job. We were excited for the income boost, but uncertain about the contract start date. Misleading promises and unexpected communication delays complicated matters. When we finally got word, we learned he was not getting paid until the end of September. Imagine that! We were already just barely making it, usually with more month than money, so how were we going to make it from July until September? We began praying in earnest for our daily bread. Our faith was tested. But then our faith is always tested in trials. Every day I breathed, *Lord, help us!*

When August arrived, we were living "on fumes." One week in and our account was down to $1.32. Like the brook, money had dried up. How would we feed our family of ten, including eight children? Discouraged to the point of despair, I clung to these promises: "But my God shall supply all your need according to his riches in glory by Christ Jesus" (Philippians 4:19 KJV) and "Because of the LORD's great love, we are not consumed, for his compassions never fail. They are new every morning; great is your faithfulness" (Lamentations 3:22–23 NIV).

At the end of our rope, we held on to hope in our God. Miraculously, He provided for us in small and big ways. Our two oldest children began voluntarily giving money from their summer earnings—to help with groceries. We got extensions from creditors and forbearance from our landlord. God provided for us in the most amazing way through longtime friends. Their generous gift was our salvation that helped us make it through September. Twenty years later, we still marvel at God's faithfulness.

If you are in a desperate place in your life, you can turn to God. "The LORD is good to those whose hope is in him" (Lamentations 3:25 NIV). You may be down to nothing, but God is up to something. Hold on! He has a door of hope for you!

REFLECTION:
Do you have a similar story? Think about how God has been faithful to you, and smile as you remember!

Suggested Scripture Reading: Lamentations 3:22–26

Our Blessed Likeness

Diane Proctor Reeder

*When God created mankind, he made them in
the likeness of God. He created them male and
female and blessed them. And he named them
"Mankind" when they were created.*

Genesis 5:1–2 NIV

In reading through the Scriptures, we find ourselves fascinated not only by God's hand, but also by His stories about
individual men and women.

We see the exploits of David, who kills lions and bears who
dare try and approach his sheep, and uses that same courage
and skill to kill one of Israel's greatest enemies, the Philistine
Goliath (1 Samuel 17:36).

We see Samson, and don't we cringe just a bit when he is
blinded and enslaved after telling the secret of his strength to
Delilah, who betrays him to the Philistines (Judges 16:30)?

Then there is Moses, who wrestles with God and argues on
behalf of His chosen people, hitting rocks and watching God
part waters, to lead more than a million Hebrews to a land of
"milk and honey" (Exodus 14:21; 33:1–17; Numbers 20:11).

And then I look at the women.

Eve, the first woman not only to give birth, but to grieve
acutely at the death of a child and to traverse the complicated
emotions that go with mothering a murderer, then give birth

to yet another child and through it all manage not to blame God (Genesis 4).

RUTH, who after the death of her husband follows his mother into a strange land, accepting Naomi's unfamiliar God as her own (Ruth 1:16) . . . then gleaning in the field to support them both and finding herself in the kind, redemptive hands of that very God whom she dared to get to know (Ruth 2:3).

And it occurs to me: to get to victory, we can look to the unique character qualities of both men and women and find ways to adapt those qualities under the guidance and the help of the Holy Spirit.

IN JESUS, we find all of these aspects in one God-man. We glimpse Him as he cries over His people, longing for them to come under His wing, comparing Himself to a mother hen (Luke 13:34–35).

Look again and there He is in the Jewish Temple, turning over carts and money-changers' tables, furious with injustice and disobedience (Luke 19:45–46).

He, as the perfect Man, is the perfect mixture of yielded submission and fierce defender of the faith.

REFLECTION:
What biblical characters do you most identify with? How do you see Jesus's character reflected in them?

Suggested Scripture Reading: Ruth 1:16; 2:2, 12–16; 4:13; Matthew 23:37; Luke 13:31–35

Unexpected Transformation

Norvella Carter

*Hypocrite! First get rid of the log in your own
eye; then you will see well enough to deal with
the speck in your friend's eye.*

MATTHEW 7:5

I remember being invited to a weeklong Christian marriage
retreat after Bill and I had been married several months.
We made plans to go together, but Bill's job sent him out
of town. I decided not to go either, because I believed that
he was the one who really needed it. Two years later, we
were invited again, this time to a seminar series for married
couples. Bill's schedule did not permit him to go, but I decided
that *I* would go and get information to share with *him*. After
all, *he* is *the one who is making all the mistakes*, I thought—and
I wanted to help *him*. Loving my husband was not as easy and
natural as I had expected it would be!

The seminar revealed much more about *me* than I cared to
hear. After my return, Bill asked, "Tell me about the seminar.
Did you enjoy it?" I was very quiet as I thought about what
I was confronted with.

How could I tell him that, based on my commune
with God in His Word, I learned I was selfish, unforgiving,
judgmental, unloving, and additionally, I held grudges?
I was so convicted that it was months before I could share
some of my seminar experiences with him, or anyone else.
I was embarrassed for anyone to know that I had miles to go
before I could relate to the Proverbs 31 wife that my grandmother esteemed so highly in our family's history. I repented

and asked the Lord to help me become a better wife, and felt remorseful that I originally thought of myself as "perfect."

A genuine transformation began to take place in me as I began to relate differently to my husband and the overall concept of marriage. I studied my Bible more intently and used the seminar materials as a guide. With thoughtful purpose, I began to practice new behaviors. My husband said it felt like he had a new wife. He began telling people that they should attend the marriage seminar even before he had attended one himself. I remember him telling a friend, "Just send your wife if you can't go . . . you won't regret it."

Since then, we've attended countless marriage classes, seminars, retreats, and trainings. After more than four decades of a successful marriage, we provide premarital counseling for our church and work with Christian couples in small fellowship groups. I continue to remember that our Lord called the person in the Scripture a "hypocrite" because there was a need to "take the plank out of their own eye" before addressing someone else's "speck" (Matthew 7:5 NKJV). I have to continually go through the process of denouncing hypocrisy and praying daily for godly attributes as related in Proverbs 31.

Marital victories may seem fewer in frequency today. Relationships take work! So many decide to "throw in the towel" at even the merest hint of trouble. The way to victory is hard, but so very worth it: we work on ourselves *first*.

REFLECTION:
What are three things you can do to be a better mate to your spouse? How do these same principles relate to your other relationships?

Suggested Scripture Reading: Proverbs 31:10–12

Moving by Faith

Juliet E. Cooper Allen

The LORD had said to Abram, "Leave your native country, your relatives, and your father's family, and go to the land that I will show you."

Genesis 12:1

Have you ever moved—across town or across the country? Every year millions of people endure this highly stressful life event, for some much more stressful and traumatic than for others.

At one time my family was moving and facing the additional stress of not having a home to move into. I can still remember that Friday when we prepared to move to a city in New York from a smaller city in Michigan. Thankfully, we had movers. The movers arrived and went right to work loading stacks of boxes and furniture into the moving van. Of course, the driver wanted to know, "What's the delivery address for this shipment?"

In the two months after my husband accepted his new position at a university, we had been searching for housing. All to no avail! With six children in tow and one on the way, we really needed a house to rent. We grew frustrated when we were unable to find anything suitable in our price range. Yet, we had committed to moving almost 500 miles away and there was no turning back. I actually thought of the faith of Abraham! I drew courage from trusting that God was going with us and ahead of us on our journey.

Remember Abraham's story? One day, God called him to leave his home in Ur of the Chaldees and go to a place He would show him (see Genesis 12). Although he had no idea where he was headed, he packed up his earthly belongings and set out on his way. Abraham trusted God and God was with him. He directed him to Canaan where he made his home. God's Word commends Abraham: "It was by faith that Abraham obeyed when God called him to leave home and go to another land that God would give him as his inheritance. He went without knowing where he was going" (Hebrews 11:8).

I encouraged myself. Surely, God would lead us to the right place for our family. He would not have provided my husband a dream job only to leave us without a place to live. With the movers set to deliver our belongings on Tuesday, we only had one day, Monday, to find a place or put everything in storage. Talk about pressure! Our backs were against the wall, but, we knew we serve the God of the breakthrough!

That very weekend, our realtor called. She had housing in our price range for us to see on Monday. In the nick of time, God had rescued us! What's more, the owners, our landlords, were a Christian family, who welcomed our family and became friends for life!

Perhaps you're facing an uncertain future. Be encouraged that God holds your future in His hands. Our Good Shepherd faithfully watches over our lives. He will provide for our needs in ways that are best for His plan and in His time, and He leads us in the way we should go as we follow Him by faith.

REFLECTION:
What are you uncertain about in your life? What can you affirm about your life in spite of that uncertainty?

Suggested Scripture Reading: Genesis 12:1–5

Caring Father

Lawrence Darmani

Your Father knows exactly what you need even before you ask him!

MATTHEW 6:8

I was only four years old as I lay by my father on a floor mat on a hot summer night. (My mother, with a baby, had her own room at the time.) This was in northern Ghana where the climate is mostly dry. Sweat covered my body, and the heat parched my throat. I felt so thirsty I shook my father awake. In the middle of that dry night, he rose up and poured water from a jar for me to quench my thirst. Throughout my life, as he did that night, he exemplified the image of a caring father. He provided what I needed.

Some of us may not have a good father figure in our life. But we all have a heavenly Father who is strong and ever-present and who does not disappoint us. Jesus taught us to pray to "our Father in heaven" (Matthew 6:9). He told us that when our daily needs confront us—food, clothing, shelter, protection (v. 31)—"your Father knows exactly what you need even before you ask him" (v. 8).

We have a Father who is always there. Night or day, whenever the going gets tough, we can trust that He will never abandon us. He has promised to care for us, and He knows better than we do what we need.

Among the topics Christ so eloquently addresses is the subject of worry. It appears that He was attuned to the fretting the human heart experiences in daily life. He encourages us to seek God's kingdom as the top priority and then we are assured our Father God will provide for us (Matthew 6:33). He suggests we manage stress by faith: "So don't worry about tomorrow, for tomorrow will bring its own worries. Today's trouble is enough for today" (v. 34).

Thank You, Lord, for the privilege of coming to
You as my Father. You know my needs before
I even ask. Thank You that You will
never turn me away.

REFLECTION:

What do you need? What do you worry about? Name it, and replace "tomorrow" in Matthew 6:34 with what you have been worrying about. Make it your daily affirmation not to worry until you have the victory over that issue.

Suggested Scripture Reading: Matthew 6:28–34

Learning to Choose

Victoria Saunders McAfee

*Jesus said, "Father, forgive them, for they don't
know what they are doing."*

Luke 23:34

I'll never forget this documentary that interrupted my
Saturday morning. At eight years old, cartoons or playing
outside had to be better than listening to someone talking
about Africa and the "Middle Passage" to slavery. But the
images kept me glued to my seat. The producers designed the
piece to educate young children. But the documentary also
launched me in learning to choose love over hate.

My view of the Motherland had been shaped by movies
like Tarzan, which depicted "stupid savages" running in fear
with spears. This brief, kid-friendly documentary paraded
before my eyes dignified kings and queens clad in royal clothing and jewels—with hair texture and skin tones like mine!
For the first time, I heard that slave traders snatched my
ancestors from a rich heritage to be brutally enslaved. I got
really angry. God's love would have to root out my bitterness.

Slavery stories planted a seed of prejudice in my heart that
blossomed into a full-blown hatred. I still attended church,
but by the time I reached junior high, I blamed people in
privileged, powerful positions for every injustice ever done to
the disadvantaged.

Thank God, another occurrence happened in junior high.
Our minister's wife, Mrs. Smith, became our youth director. She had one goal in mind: everyone in our youth group
should know and receive Jesus as Lord and Savior.

I'd taken my dunk in the baptismal pool and thought *I'm heaven bound because I'm little miss goody two shoes*. Mrs. Smith blew up my neatly packaged theory. She made Ephesians 2:8–9 clear; it's by grace, not our effort, we are saved. Jesus died on the cross for our sins; trust in Him for salvation. He alone is our entrance into heaven. God opened my heart to receive Jesus.

As I grew in this relationship with Christ, He made it plain that unforgiveness, bitterness, and hatred could not share the same heart in love with Him. He revealed how Christians and well-meaning people of a different skin color from mine risked their lives for slaves' freedom and participated in the Civil Rights Movement.

I learned about forgiveness in Joseph's life (Genesis 50:20). I heard about the response of Stephen while being stoned to death (Acts 7:60). And one verse I heard repeatedly, spoken by Jesus as He hung on the cross and forgave His murderers (Luke 23:34). In each instance, God's people refused to allow themselves to be captured in the prison of unforgiveness. Instead they embraced God's love and chose to pour it out on the undeserving.

> *Lord, search my heart, today. I want to release*
> *anyone I'm holding in my inner prison*
> *of unforgiveness.*

REFLECTION:
"Forgiveness doesn't mean you excuse the crime. It only means you're no longer willing to be the victim." Nelson Mandela

Suggested Scripture Reading: Genesis 50:20; Acts 7:60; Luke 23:34

Trust God!

Shirley A. June

*Trust in the LORD with all your heart and lean
not on your own understanding; in all your ways
submit to him, and he will make your paths
straight.*

Proverbs 3:5–6 NIV

It was winter. Patches of snow stood here and there on the
frozen ground. It was one of those cold stark days in late
December when all you'd want to do was stay inside if you
had a choice. Inside, boxes, baby beds, and a few remaining
piles of "to-be-loaded" items lay in the midst of furniture that
was to be left behind. It was finally the day to head South
to warmth, and my husband's six-month study at a divinity
school. We were trying to fit the move between two holidays
and avoid Christmas and New Year's traffic rush.

Following several action-packed days, we thought we were
finally within minutes of leaving! Instead, a problem with the
rental truck required returning it to the company for repair.
Another day brought another surprise when our second truck
did not tow properly.

Nothing ever happens the way you want, does it? We
found ourselves going from excitement to frustration to
"should we even be doing this at all?" Finally, my husband
decided we'd just go with what we could take in the car, ship
the books, and leave everything else home!

On the road the next day, we encountered snow, snail-
paced low-visibility traffic for miles, and saw many abandoned vehicles off the road! We shuddered to think what it

might have been like for us had we been in the moving truck towing a car. We thanked God that those difficulties resulted in revamping our travel plans. Disappointment proved a "blessing in disguise"!

We never know what blessings God has for us that are wrapped in the cloak of disappointment, frustrated plans, and even so-called failure. Instead of looking at the cloak, let us challenge ourselves to look at what is underneath: God's purposes, working and weaving out the tapestry of our lives in ways that we will later look back on as miraculous. Trust Him, no matter what clothes your circumstances may be wearing.

REFLECTION:
After all the times that God shows us that His way is best—all of the disappointments that turned out to be blessings, all of the detours that catapult us into new experiences—what is it that causes us to doubt His ways?

Suggested Scripture Reading: 2 Samuel 22:3; Proverbs 3:5–6; 1 Timothy 6:17

How Can We Sing?

Michelle Loyd-Paige

But how can we sing the songs of the Lord while in a pagan land?

Psalm 137:4

My last trip to the continent of Africa was to the country of Tanzania. It was my first time to East Africa, and I was attending the Theological Education for Africa (TEA) conference. The conference, a gathering of 530 African pastors, lasted five days, and every morning, afternoon, and evening there was Christ-centered, lively worship. A praise team comprised of four African pastors led us in congregational songs, some in English and some in *Kiswahili*. A choir from a local Christian college sang and danced with such high, celebratory energy that it was hard not to jump into the aisle and dance along with them—and sometimes we did. It was announced over and over again that "when Africans come together, we sing and dance."

Just before one of the afternoon sessions, something unexpected happened. I and the other three African Americans in attendance were asked to come to the stage. We went to the stage not knowing what to expect. The conference host proceeded to "welcome us home."

There was great cheering and clapping from those gathered and tears in the eyes of us on the stage. In that moment, I could not help but think of my ancestors who, according to my DNA testing, are from Cameroon, Congo, Benin, Togo, Mali, and Senegal. I'd like to think that they were kings and queens before coming to America. Captured and enslaved, they were not yet Americans when they arrived. No one was "welcoming them home." Psalm 137:1–4 (NIV) comes to mind as I think of what it must have felt like:

> *By the rivers of Babylon we sat and wept when we remembered Zion. There on the poplars we hung our harps, for there our captors asked us for songs, our tormentors demanded songs of joy; they said, "Sing us one of the songs of Zion!" How can we sing the songs of the LORD while in a foreign land?*

Like the Jewish exiles in Psalm 137, Africans were taken and enslaved. The heaviness that the Africans felt as they thought of home must have been similar to that felt by the Jews as they thought of Zion. *Sing? How? Why? Certainly not to please our captors,* they must have thought.

Nevertheless, eventually, we the descendants of African slaves did sing. Not to please our captors, but to please the God who saved us. "Come, let us sing for joy to the LORD; let us shout aloud to the Rock of our salvation. Let us come before him with thanksgiving and extol him with music and song (Psalm 95:1–2 NIV). We have learned to sing in a land that was "foreign" (Psalm 137:4 NIV) to our ancestors and, at times, can still feel foreign today. We sing songs of lament, songs of joy, songs of resistance, songs of hope, and songs of celebration. We sing, as the blood of our African ancestors runs through our veins. We sing!

REFLECTION:
What gospel songs bring you comfort when you feel like you are in a "foreign" land?

Suggested Scripture Reading: Psalms 95, 100

A Time to Act

David McCasland

"If anyone thirsts, let him come to Me and drink.
He who believes in Me, as the Scripture has said,
out of his heart will flow rivers of living water."
JOHN 7:37–38 NKJV

US Congressman John Lewis was twenty-three years old when he participated in the historic 1963 civil rights "March on Washington" led by Dr. Martin Luther King Jr. Half a century later, journalist Bill Moyers asked Lewis how he was affected by Dr. King's "I Have A Dream" speech that day.

Mr. Lewis replied, "You couldn't leave after hearing him speak and go back to business as usual. You had to do something, you had to act. You had to move. You had to go out and spread the good news."

Similarly, many who encountered Jesus found it impossible to remain neutral about Him. John 7:25–46 records two different reactions to Jesus. While "many of the people believed in Him" (v. 31), the religious leaders tried to silence Him by sending temple guards to arrest Him (v. 32). The guards were likely present when Jesus said, "If anyone thirsts, let him come to Me and drink. He who believes in Me, as the Scripture has said, out of his heart will flow rivers of living water" (vv. 37–38). The guards returned without Jesus and were asked, "Why have you not brought Him?" (v. 45). They answered, "No man ever spoke like this Man!" (v. 46).

The words of Jesus compel us to act, and to move, beyond business as usual.

So let our lips and lives express
The holy gospel we profess;
So let our works and virtues shine,
To prove the doctrine all divine.

—Watts

REFLECTION:
Jesus's death forgives my past sins and inspires my present obedience.

Suggested Scripture Reading: Isaiah 7:37–46

BRACE OF GRACE

COKIESHA B. ROBINSON

*And give thanks for everything to God the Father
in the name of our Lord Jesus Christ.*

EPHESIANS 5:20

It's always great to be thankful. On a holiday, special day, any day. We see social media "thank" posts daily for: relationship with Christ, health, family and friends, jobs, ministries, opened doors and opportunities, dreams realized, homes and warmth and shelter, food, peace, freedom, safety, and the list goes on.

My prayer is that gratefulness will extend beyond Thanksgiving weekend or another holiday season and remain my attitude and lifestyle. All that we have, if we are honest, is more than enough. We should pause often to give thanks for who God is and for who He has made us to be. Every hair, fingerprint, dimple, freckle, personality trait, and strength each of us has is designed to reflect God's image (Genesis 1:27).

As we mature, life's setbacks, strains, and struggles bring blessings and testimonies we can be grateful for too. Devastation, failure, betrayal, loss, and hurt turn our hearts in closer intimacy with His. He knows what the hurts He allows will produce. "That I may know Him, . . . and the fellowship of His sufferings" (Philippians 3:10 KJV) tells us that intimacy will involve suffering. Suffering can produce growth in patience, hope, forgiveness, humility, and resilience for Christ. The apostle Paul testified, "Therefore I am well content with weaknesses, with insults, with distresses, with persecutions, with difficulties, for Christ's sake; for when I am weak, then I am strong" (2 Corinthians 12:10 NASB).

A layoff, diagnosis, death, loss of mate, or end of friendship can sour our lives. So can feeling overwhelmed or discontent. There's good news! "He will never leave you nor forsake you." (Deuteronomy 31:6 NIV). He not only walks with us on the mountains but also in the valleys of our experiences.

Many "walks" support cures for breast cancer, diabetes, AIDS, and other life-altering diseases. I saw a sign once: "Limping is still walking." It encouraged runners, joggers, and walkers to stay in the race even if they were limping. Limping means we may walk slower, find a new perspective and norm, but it means we have not quit or become consumed by defeat or depression. Limps still reflect God's grace.

A few months before my wedding, I experienced a life-changing mission trip to Izmir, Turkey, While studying the seven churches of Asia Minor, our group also built relationships with people and shared Christ. Then I had an accident and injured my legs, ankles, knees, and feet, returning to the States with a limp and a testimony. On my wedding day, I had a knee brace under my wedding gown. It didn't stop me from a wonderful time, walking down the aisle to the man of my dreams, greeting guests, and dancing the night away. My struggle changed me but didn't cripple me.

Dear Lord, allow our suffering to strengthen us.
Thank You for victory over all things.

REFLECTION:
What are you thankful for? What has changed your life and reminds you of God's grace? Take a moment and praise God for His "brace" of grace on your life.

Suggested Scripture Reading: Choose a portion of Psalm 119.

Powerful Peacemakers

Xochitl E. Dixon

*God blesses those who work for peace, for they
will be called the children of God.*

Matthew 5:9

As an acclaimed educator, champion of human equality, and a member of the NAACP, Dr. Mary McLeod Bethune defied societal limitations. She founded what is now Bethune-Cookman University—one of today's top twenty historically Black colleges and universities. She rose above obstacles and triumphed over discrimination to serve alongside great men like President Hoover, President Coolidge, and W. E. B. DuBois. Shattering stereotypes, she became a trusted advisor on minority affairs to US President Franklin D. Roosevelt and developed a close friendship with Eleanor Roosevelt.

At the age of seventy-eight, Dr. Bethune displayed courageous transparency and wisdom when she wrote "My Last Will and Testament." She expressed "joy and great satisfaction" in knowing her "long career of fruitful toil" had helped many people, though she admitted the expanse of the work still required to realize her greatest dream—full equality.

Devoted to life as a peacemaker, Dr. Bethune believed loving our neighbors meant "being interracial, interreligious, and international." She declared faith in God as "the greatest power" and dedicated her life to building bridges as she longed for "a world of Peace, Progress, Brotherhood, and Love." Penning powerful words with confidence and humility, she proclaimed love "is more beneficial than hate." She inspired others to stand together to celebrate diversity and cultivate a community built on "faith, courage, brotherhood, dignity, ambition, and responsibility."

Though she'd endured and witnessed *great* prejudice, she refused to allow bitterness to restrain her or seek revenge for the pains of injustice, discrimination, and hatred. She *did not* minimize, justify, or excuse offenders or the magnitude of their offenses. Instead, she demonstrated extraordinary strength and deep dependence on God's trustworthy sovereignty and healing goodness when she said: "Forgiving is not about forgetting, it's letting go of the hurt."

Dr. Bethune served selflessly, accomplished great things by embracing God's standard of living, and exemplified the Beatitudes (Matthew 5:1–12). She relied on the Lord as she battled hate with love and placed the needs of others above her own (v. 3). She endured persecution and trials, affirming that meekness is not weakness (v. 5). Committed to a life of godliness and forbearance while working toward justice, she showed her appreciation for the mercy she had received from the Lord by extending compassion and clemency toward others (vv. 6–7). As a true ambassador for Christ, she remained focused on the eternal rewards of a righteous life lived by faith (vv. 8–10), followed Jesus no matter what the personal cost, and kept her hope fixed on His promises (vv. 11–12).

In her "Last Will and Testament," this courageous woman of God confirmed her commitment to abolishing hatred and discrimination, as she combatted injustice by abiding by the Beatitudes with bold confidence. We, too, can work together in love and unity until we realize her greatest dream—total equality. As we honor Dr. Mary McLeod Bethune's legacy, we can persevere in victory as powerful peacemakers and change the world by loving like Jesus—the Prince of Peace.

*Lord, please empower us to serve together as
Your representatives, working in peace and
unity as we trust You to change our world by
helping us love and respect You and all our
neighbors. In Jesus's name, Amen.*

REFLECTION:
Christ's love empowers us to live in peace as we triumph over hate.

Suggested Scripture Reading: Matthew 5:1–12

Are We There Yet?

Diane Proctor Reeder

*So, my dear brothers and sisters, be strong and
immovable. Always work enthusiastically for the
Lord, for you know that nothing you do for the
Lord is ever useless.*

1 Corinthians 15:58

Rest and work: the typical God-paradox! We rest in Him
(Psalm 37:7), but we are "always abounding in the
word of the Lord, knowing that our labour is not in vain"
(1 Corinthians 15:58 KJV).

This, then, is the victory: We rest in the sovereignty of
God, knowing that God does not depend on us to perform
His mighty acts. He merely invites us to participate.

Sometimes His invitation is a soft whisper, a polite gentleman holding out his hand:

> *And, behold, the LORD passed by, and a great and
> strong wind rent the mountains, and brake in
> pieces the rocks before the LORD; but the LORD
> was not in the wind: and after the wind an
> earthquake; but the LORD was not in the earth-
> quake: And after the earthquake a fire; but the
> LORD was not in the fire: and after the fire a still
> small voice* (1 Kings 19:11–13 KJV).

Sometimes it is all fire and smoke and raging sea:

The heathen raged, the kingdoms were moved: he uttered his voice, the earth melted (Psalm 46:6 KJV).

Either way, He gives us the choice. As we read the Scriptures, it seems that this is the pattern: He acts like a gentleman when He senses we are ready to listen. He rages with fire when we are in an uproar, yelling too loud to hear. I am thinking here of David, who blatantly committed adultery and murder until Nathan snatched him up with a story that angered him so much until David realized that the story was about himself (2 Samuel 12:1–13). To me, that is God roaring.

Then I consider the poor rich young ruler who came to Jesus with the question, "How can I live forever?" and Jesus, far from berating him, gave him a quiet challenge to sell everything and give it away to the poor (Matthew 19:21). His message, tough. His words and demeanor, soft.

Either way, He does not depend on us. We need not take up that cross—He already has! We need only to come in response to His invitation, partake, and then work His works while we are still in this world.

REFLECTION:
When was the last time you felt *rest* in the Lord? When will you go back?

Suggested Scripture Reading: Matthew 11:28; John 9:4

THE WHISPER

DEBORAH FOX

What I tell you now in the darkness, shout abroad when daybreak comes. What I whisper in your ear, shout from the housetops for all to hear!

MATTHEW 10:27

The night weighs heavy upon me. In the darkness, I'm alone;
and the urges surge through me as constant as a drone.
It calls to me, continuously! I ignore and don't obey
but it yells from a hell I cannot dispel;
it's too potent to my dismay.

I try to resist; make it cease and desist, to rid the fiend within.
And I fight, with all my might to overwrite, but it always seems to win.
Fiend wins. My head spins. I'm confined and I'm pinned
to this spiral down into the deep. As I rotate and wait
and the cycle abates, I hear my soul and it weeps.

My self-inflicted affliction has made its prediction:
I'll never be whole again.
My dereliction has caused my addiction; and I suffer in the pain.
I succumb. Now I'm numb;
Fiend's chum I've become, my countenance glum
I can't abstain from the Fiend's mighty drum.

What can touch my nothing-ness and give to me a hope, no less;
allow me to live a life blessed? Nothing can, is my guess.
A Whisper; my soul awoke. Was it a voice I heard? Who spoke?

What I heard, I thought absurd.
I was trapped and chained and locked.
There were doors all around but
Fiend had me bound and all exits blocked.
A Whispered shout, "Get up! Get out!
Crawl on the floor to the door!
Your life I'll restore as I swore from before;
get up!" the Whisper implored.

I crawled but I couldn't. My body just wouldn't,
'cause of things I shouldn't have done.
I lay there, spent, in Fiend's arms malcontent;
it just wouldn't relent. We were one.
Fiend was Devourer, to nothing would cower,
over me it did tower and rule.
The Whisper was Power, it devoured Devourer;
Power towered over the ghoul.

Fiend was defeated. Its hold was depleted;
I could clearly make a choice.
Lay with the ghoul and allow it to rule
or walk with Whisper's voice.

The Whisper speaks so mild and meek; my soul awakes, awakened.
I hear in my ear a message so dear, "You'll never be forsaken."
I'd been unaware the Whisper's been there, tolerant and enduring.
The Whisper is Love, sent from above, operant and reassuring.

The Whisper said, "Live. Your sins I'll forgive; I love you. Come to me."
And that very night, I stood up—upright, prepared for victory.
My guess was all wrong. I'm where I belong;
in the bosom of the King.

and the gift He has gifted has my heart uplifted;
I hear my soul, now it sings.

I'm not tempest tossed or amongst those who are lost.
I stand on firm foundation.
Urges still surge then
The Whisper emerges, and I rest in my salvation.

REFLECTION:
Have you ever heard God's "whisper"? What did He say to
your spirit?

Suggested Scripture Reading: Deuteronomy 31:1–7;
Matthew 10:1–16, 26–27; 11:28–30

A Cloud of Witnesses

B. Williams Waters

"This is where *my* grandparents lived," Granddaddy said, pointing to the newly furrowed acres of land. "My parents lived there," he said, pointing farther up the lane.

Granddaddy and I spent the day driving around the countryside. We visited the old cemetery. He showed me where the schoolhouse once stood and the hilltop site of the old church. Silently, we stood there on the hill looking down into a gently sloping valley. In the breeze, I could "hear" the call of the church bell and "see" the people "walking" up the slope as they gathered for church. And, in that moment, I felt a strong connection with the people of the past. I knew of their faith; I had taught about it. I knew of their strength; I had seen it. I knew their God.

Between Hebrews 11:1 and Hebrews 12:1 stands a roll call of faith. These verses offer testimony *of* the faithful *to* the faithfulness of God.

Looking back on that day, standing on that hill with my grandfather, I see my "cloud of witnesses." Granddaddy and his father before him were witnesses; his sons, my uncles—preachers; my brother, a preacher; my grandmother, a preacher; my son, a preacher. But, the roll does not end here. My parents, Bishop and Naomi, Uncle Mac, Aunt Delphine, Aunt Geneva, and Aunt Bertha, and on and on, were witnesses. Some of them are still here and others gone, but they still watch "from the grandstands," urging me on.

REFLECTION: Who are the people and what are the testimonies of those whose witness encourages you?

Suggested Scripture Reading: Hebrews 11–12

TEACHERS MUST BE HUMBLE TO LEARN

For our hope is in the living God, who is the
Savior of all people and particularly of all believers. . . .
Keep a close watch on how you live and on your teaching.
Stay true to what is right for the sake of your own salvation
and the salvation of those who hear you.
—1 TIMOTHY 4:10, 16

False teachers had distorted the gospel in the Ephesian church as documented in Paul's first letter to Timothy (1 Timothy 1:3–7; 6:3–5). They were not interested in learning—they had "turned their backs on the truth" (1 Timothy 6:5). But Paul had taught Timothy the truth, and Paul wrote a second letter to Timothy to encourage the young man to pass the truth on faithfully to others.

A *Changana* proverb from Mozambique says, *Loku ungha tsamanga u djondza, ungha yimi u djondzissa,* meaning, "If you do not sit down to learn, do not stand up to teach." Teachers must be people who are humble enough to study, like Timothy. As you grow and gain maturity and experience, you can teach others from what you have learned. Although Timothy was young, he had learned the faith from his mother and grandmother (2 Timothy 1:5) and been taught by Paul (2 Timothy 1:13–14). **The greater the position of leadership we hold or want to hold, the more we need to be learning by reading books, meeting with mentors, and studying God's Word.**

—*Africa Study Bible* commentary on 2 Timothy

PART THREE

JAN SPIVEY GILCHRIST

LEGACY

Sword and Shield

Diane Proctor Reeder

And he shall judge among the nations, and shall rebuke many people: and they shall beat their swords into plowshares, and their spears into pruninghooks: nation shall not lift up sword against nation, neither shall they learn war any more.

Isaiah 2:4 KJV

I'm gonna lay down my sword and shield, down by the riverside . . . ain't gonna study war no more."

I love how our ancestors turned Scripture into song! They seemed to boil God's Word down to the essence of the message, making their own life applications along the way. When I think about this particular passage in Isaiah, I immediately go to the New Testament and reflect on how our weapons are not made by hands, but are spiritual ones, mighty and infinitely more effective than anything I could dream up (2 Corinthians 10:4).

This is a tribute to their brilliance . . . to how, despite their challenges with literacy and language, they found ways to make the Scriptures their own, embedded with messages particular to their life circumstances:

Sword and shield

(my own)

sword and shield

I thee lay down

Tired of fighting battles

(my own)
Down by the river
where the water rushes clean
all glinty in the sun
water that washes away grief (my own)
and anger (my own)
down by the river
lets me forget sadness and regret
leaving remembrances
scrubbed clean
letting me pick up
sword and shield
(not my own)
stand
and watch the redeeming
unfold.

REFLECTION:
What are the human "swords and shields" in your life?

Suggested Scripture Reading: Exodus 14:13; Isaiah 2:4;
Ephesians 6:13

Thanks for Waiting

Michael T. Westbrook

Lazy people are soon poor; hard workers get rich.
PROVERBS 10:4

When you walked into the office waiting room of Progressive Cab, you were greeted with this logo-sign on the wall above the counter: "Thanks for Waiting 22 Years." On the counter itself was a box of giveaways for customers; pencils and pens carrying the cab company logo statement.

Anyone inquiring about the meaning of the logo heard Mr. Dickins, the owner, proudly tell his story. As an African American who started his cab business in a small suburban community, he had had to overcome many obstacles to get started—and to keep his company going while trying to take care of his family. It took decades!

Starting with one car, an office in a back alley, and a telephone, his continued effort and perseverance paid off. Eventually, he owned a fleet of fifteen cars with drivers operating from six o'clock a.m. until midnight, and an office with waiting room located inside the town's train station.

Paul the apostle admonishes all Christ-followers, "Let us not become weary in doing good, for at the proper time we will reap a harvest if we do not give up" (Galatians 6:9 NIV). Paul is telling us that if we keep going in spite of any obstacles that we may encounter, there is a time already set aside to receive our reward. He speaks here about "doing good" in the faith, but the principle still holds. *All hard work brings a profit,* God tells us through King Solomon (Proverbs 14:23 NIV). That's refreshing news to those of us who are in the midst of heavy burdens and challenges that life throws at us. Even when it gets so hard and it doesn't seem like we can take another step, we know that there is a reward coming. Whether we are working to provide for our families or working in our communities and churches, the principle holds. The reward may be material. The reward may be spiritual. But there *will* be a reward!

As believers we face many things as we attempt to run this Christian race and it can become tiring. Don't give up because there is a reward waiting for those that don't grow weary. So if you're working real hard to sow into a business, ministry, or other venture that just seems like it will never get where you want it to be, keep on working at it with the anticipation of hanging your own "sign on the wall." The only question you need to ask is, "What will my sign say?"

REFLECTION:
Write down what you would like your "sign" to say when you get to where you believe God is taking you.

Suggested Scripture Reading: Psalm 27:14; Proverbs 10:4; Isaiah 40:31

The Last Supper

Anita Patterson

On the first day of the Festival of Unleavened Bread, the disciples came to Jesus and asked, "Where do you want us to make preparations for you to eat the Passover?"

MATTHEW 26:17 NIV

As a child, I remember being awakened by the smells of buttery homemade biscuits and sizzling bacon. They are memories I will never forget. My great-grandmother and grandmother passed down to us the importance of having family meals together. We would have three meals a day; breakfast, lunch, and dinner. It's funny because as soon as we finished eating breakfast and cleaning up, it was time for lunch and it was the same pattern for dinner. Auntie Corene would make her specialty baked macaroni and cheese. "And, nobody else better not make it!" My siblings and cousins and I sat at the kiddy table while the adults were in the dining room having a good time.

Generations later, we are still implementing that same value and tradition of togetherness in our extended families. When we sit around a table for family gatherings, we bless our food and the rich, nourishing conversations full of laughter, encouragement—and, at times, sorrow—begin.

Jesus connected with His disciples and other close friends around a meal. There was teaching, laughter, encouragement, and prayer. Coming together around a meal was important to Jesus because it gave Him the opportunity to impart wisdom and knowledge to those He encountered. In Luke, we learn that "Martha was distracted by all the preparations that had to be made. She came to him and asked, 'Lord, don't you care that my sister has left me to do the work by myself? Tell her to help me!'" (Luke 10:40 NIV).

I guess Martha was distracted by preparing her collard greens, frying chicken, whipping together banana pudding, and setting the table. She lost sight of the real meaning of the fellowship, and Jesus reminded her what was important. We don't want to get too engulfed in preparing the meal that we spend the entire time in the kitchen. Take that apron off and connect with the family and friends (the dishes can wait). Share what God is doing in your life, give encouragement, and offer spiritual advice where needed.

Even before Jesus went to the cross, He valued His last meal with the disciples. He reminded them to come together as often as they could to commune with one another, and to celebrate Communion in remembrance of Him (Luke 22:19).

When you sit around a table with family and friends, remember those who have imparted wisdom and spiritual guidance in your life. Family legacies are so important. What legacies do you remember that you want to continue in your family? Even better: start a new tradition and create a legacy for others to continue.

REFLECTION:
Thank God for the legacies He left for us to follow in His Word. What new legacies has the Lord placed on your heart to start in your family?

Suggested Scripture Reading: Psalm 78:4; Psalm 145:4; Revelation 3:20

Passionate Pursuit

Lee N. June

But let justice roll on like a river, righteousness like a never-failing stream.

Amos 5:24 NIV

For those of us who were alive and attuned to the Civil Rights Movement in the 1960s, we witnessed individuals who exemplified lifestyles of justice. Dr. Martin Luther King Jr., Reverend Ralph Abernathy, and Fannie Lou Hamer, among others, are included in this group. Whether or not you were alive during the 1960s, all of us can vicariously witness and experience as we read the Scriptures and see in the prophets and Jesus this same commitment. They exemplified the urging of the Old Testament prophet Micah "to act justly and to love mercy and to walk humbly with your God" (Micah 6:8 NIV).

Take a moment to meditate on those verses from Amos and Micah, as well as this one:

> *"What sorrow awaits you teachers of religious law and you Pharisees. Hypocrites! For you are careful to tithe even the tiniest income from your herb gardens, but you ignore the more import-ant aspects of the law—justice, mercy, and faith. You should tithe, yes, but do not neglect the more important things"* (Matthew 23:23).

Then imagine yourself living a life and lifestyle fully commit-ted to justice. How does this feel? What things might you have to change in order to live that way?

The three meditation passages deserve our regular attention and reflection. Prominent in the Old Testament and continuing in the New Testament is God's desire for His people to treat others justly and ensure that society is overflowing and embedded with justice.

These passages and the Bible, in general, make it clear that justice is to be a lifetime passion—a passion that leads to action. Note that Amos says we are to "let justice roll on like a river"; that Micah says that we are to "act justly"; and Jesus says that justice is what the scribes and Pharisees "should have practiced." All of them indicate that justice is a lifestyle, a continuous action. It is not something to simply desire or wish for—rather it is what we *do*.

My definition of justice is rendering (doing) unto others on a continuous basis that which is due to them according to God's biblical standards. What a nation and world there would be if all of us as Christians devoted our lives to doing justice. Indeed, what a wonderful world this would be!

Lord, thank You that You are a God of justice.
You have provided us the resources and tools to
do justice and live lives of justice. Help us in
our daily lives and activities to rely on You,
Your Word, and the Holy Spirit in committing
ourselves to doing justice, loving mercy, and
walking humbly with You every day.

REFLECTION:
Reflect on the meanings of the word *justice*. What goes through your mind? Write down your response(s).

Suggested Scripture Reading: Isaiah 1:17; Amos 5:24; Micah 6:8

GRANDMA'S WORDS

DIANE PROCTOR REEDER

Therefore, since we are surrounded by such a huge crowd of witnesses to the life of faith, let us strip off every weight that slows us down, especially the sin that so easily trips us up. And let us run with endurance the race God has set before us.

HEBREWS 12:1

Have you ever seen my mother's black book?" my mother casually mentioned to me as we sat in the living room, talking after the death of my father. "No," I replied, wondering how it was that she never thought to tell me about it.

I did have a vague recollection of her telling me that Grandma Floyd had kept a list of every book she'd ever read. I eagerly took the black book, a binder, really, filled with the most exquisite handwriting. *That's where Mom and I got our excellent penmanship from,* I thought.

Grandma Floyd, she told me, had written in the book over the course of her life. I wanted to look at it myself, take the words in. But Mom wanted to read it to me herself. Her voice cracked a little as she read some of the prayers.

I finally got to read the book list—and what a list! Classics by the US authors Dreiser and Thurber and by the Russian author Dostoyevsky. Titles familiar but intriguing. *And poetry.* Grandma wrote about her son, and of war and death, and the importance of kindness and the sufficiency of her Savior. She wrote of love. Her words were melancholy—whether they were hers or copied from others—and reminded me of my own. But most importantly, the most soaring prayers. Here is just one:

> Dear Heavenly Father,
>
> As I read over the beautiful 23rd Psalm, how can I ever doubt thee—how can I ever worry about the future? Thou art always with me. Thou hast brought me thus far and Thou will be with me all the days of my life. Thine own Son Jesus said unto us: "Take no thought saying, what shall we eat? Or what shall we drink? Or wherewithal shall we be clothed: For your Heavenly Father knoweth ye have need of all these things. But seek ye first the kingdom of God, and his righteousness; and all these things shall be added unto you."
>
> (Matthew 6:31–33).

For me, this small, light-filled moment of connection was yet another expansion of what Paul in the book of Hebrews calls "a cloud of witnesses" (Hebrews 12:1 KJV). A delightful expansion, a gift from the grave, given by a faith-filled grandmother that let me know once again, in yet another blessed way, that I am not alone.

REFLECTION:
Have you ever asked your parents about their parents' experiences? What have you learned, and how do their stories affect you?

Suggested Scripture Reading: Hebrews 12:1–3

Good Gifts

Juliet E. Cooper Allen

So if you sinful people know how to give good gifts to your children, how much more will your heavenly Father give good gifts to those who ask him.

MATTHEW 7:11

"What do you want for your birthday?" Being a mom of eight, I have asked that question more times than I can count. As a parent, I always wanted to wow my children with a special gift, one he or she would love. Usually, that meant a trip to Toys R Us or another chain. With eight birthdays to prepare for and celebrate each year, there were many trips to the toy store. Despite my husband's lament about his wallet, we always found a way to celebrate our children in this way.

While teaching about prayer in His Sermon on the Mount, Jesus confirmed that parents naturally desire to bless their children. "Which of you, if your son asks for bread, will give him a stone? Or if he asks for a fish, will give him a snake?" (Matthew 7:9–10 NIV). Jesus knew that parents want the best for their children and would not give them what is harmful or bad.

Consequently, every year, parents buy gifts, especially toys, for their children. Toys that break, get lost, or get tossed aside in favor of newer ones. These material gifts have a limited lifespan. What if we decided to enhance our gift giving and focus on gifts that stand the test of time, build wisdom in their lives, and prepare them for eternity? What if we give them gifts that cannot be bought in a store or online? Valuable gifts that do not cost any money but demand a *spiritual* commitment?

Suppose we start with faith? Our children need faith because they will not see God without it. We cannot *give* them faith, per se, but we can create an environment for faith to take root and grow. Teaching Scripture, praying with and for them, and worshiping together will point their hearts towards God.

Then add to faith, hope. Hope is sustaining grace that enables us to persevere in the trials and storms of life. By cultivating a spirit of hope, our children will have this gift to anchor their souls when they face adversity. Then they can "be joyful in hope, patient in affliction, faithful in prayer" (Romans 12:12 NIV).

We should introduce them to God's love. "For God so loved the world that he gave his one and only Son, that whoever believes in him shall not perish but have eternal life" (John 3:16 NIV). God's love is unconditional and fits every heart. That love will never fail them.

The next time you and I plan on giving a gift to our child, we can remember faith, hope, and love. Faith inspires, hope sustains, and love redeems. These perfect gifts come from our heavenly Father. What's more, they are priceless and bring eternal dividends!

REFLECTION:
What are concrete ways that adults can encourage this in all children: faith, hope, and love?

Suggested Scripture Reading: Matthew 7:11; Hebrews 11:6; James 1:17

Tough and Tender

Diane Proctor Reeder

*And you must commit yourselves wholeheartedly
to these commands that I am giving you today.
Repeat them again and again to your children.
Talk about them when you are at home and
when you are on the road, when you are going to
bed and when you are getting up.*

Deuteronomy 6:6–7

My grandfather was born in Georgia in 1897. He came
North in the Great Migration of African Americans who
were looking for opportunity with a new and fast-growing business
known as Ford Motor company. He worked in the coal
mines as a child and grew strong enough to brave the work
phenomenon known as "shakeout," where he had to handle
heavy, large ladles of hot, molten metal all while managing
not to kill himself in the safety-challenged auto plants of the
1920s and thirties. My mother loves to brag about how he
would come home from work with his bad back, go upstairs,
and scream in agony after holding in his pain all day.

He was tough, a trait he passed on to his four children and
six grandchildren.

So why is it that I have a singular memory that seems to
contradict that toughness?

"Grandpa," I would say as a young girl, "Do Little Jack."

"Little Jack," written by Eugene Hall, was a long story-
poem about a poverty-stricken boy who lived "on the friend-
less street." He had tattered pants, a torn hat, no shoes, and
no shirt. But he did a deed that would, in the eyes of the poet

and my grandpa, forever endear him to the "stars in heaven."

He saved a little toddler from an oncoming train. Little Jack ran like the wind to toss the boy from the track, but "A slip! A cry! The train rolls by/Brave 'Little Jack' is lost."

The first time grandpa recited the poem in its entirety to me, I cried. Every time I asked him to recite it, the tears would fall anew, just as if I were hearing it for the first time.

One Christmas, I decided I would find the poem, and print and frame it, using my granddad's headshot as a watermark. I wanted to memorialize this special time and pass its message of self-sacrifice and love to the next generation: my cousin's children as well as my own.

I had my sister read it at Christmastime. Not a dry eye in the house. Even better: everyone in the family remembered that poem. Grandpa had recited it for all of us. I never even knew.

"Write the word on your foreheads," the Scriptures tell us (see Deuteronomy 6:8). We are to tell God's words to our children and our children's children, so they will not forget. This poem, I am sure, was a message sent by God Himself, a divine parable told through the rough, coal-mined, factory-ravaged body of a grandfather who knew that living with an eye toward heaven is what really matters.

REFLECTION:

What can you remember from your childhood that was really significant to your spiritual life and perspective? How has that shaped you?

Suggested Scripture Reading: Deuteronomy 6:6–8; John 15:13

Growing Like Jesus

Lee N. June

*And Jesus grew in wisdom and stature, and in
favor with God and Man.*

Luke 2:52 NIV

Most of us grow up admiring certain people. This type of admiration is a natural human tendency. Some individuals we admire end up being our role models and possibly mentors. As I was growing up, some of my early role models were my father (Lawson), mother (Harriett), some deacons in the church, and certain schoolteachers. Later, national figures like Dr. Martin Luther King Jr. and Reverend Tom Skinner, as well as pastors like Reverend James Offutt Sr., Reverend Dr. Lloyd Blue, Reverend Ferdinand Fritz, and Dr. Willie Richardson—they are all inspirations to me. They were the embodiment of Paul's admonition:

> *In your relationships with one another, have the same mindset as Christ Jesus, Who being in very nature God, did not consider equality with God something to be used to his own advantage; rather, he made himself nothing by taking he very nature of a servant, being made in human likeness* (Philippians 2:5–7 NIV).

The individuals that were my role models had attributes such as kindness, concern for others, integrity, and boldness. They were encouragers, had the ability to motivate, and were hopeful about the future.

The role model for all Christians is Jesus Christ. While He is the Savior and Lord, Jesus Christ is also that model for us to grow in our humanity as He grew in His. Note the four areas in which Luke says of Jesus that He "increased" (KJV).

According to Luke, Jesus Christ grew in stature, in wisdom, in favor with God, and in favor with humanity. We, too, can and are to grow in these areas. Stature or physical growth is the easiest of the four and is largely biologically determined. It can also be enhanced by diet, exercise, rest, and other ways of taking care of our bodies. For wisdom, we can ask God for it and follow His precepts. To grow in *favor* with God and humanity, we need to have the mind of Christ, as well as read, study, and follow God's blueprint for life: the Bible.

> *Lord Jesus, thank You for dying on the cross for us. Thank You that You modelled for us how to grow and in what dimensions. Help us to have Your mindset and to grow not only in stature, but also in wisdom, in favor with You, and in favor with our fellow humanity.*

REFLECTION:
Think of individuals important to you, that you consider role models or inspirations. Reflect on why; what attributes or characteristics do they possess?

Suggested Scripture Reading: 1 Corinthians 1:11; Philippians 2:5–7

THE ULTIMATE MISSIONARY

MARIA WESTBROOK

However, I consider my life worth nothing to me; my only aim is to finish the race and complete the task the Lord Jesus has given me—the task of testifying to the good news of God's grace.

ACTS 20:24 NIV

Everywhere we turn, we hear of someone in crisis: family, friends, neighbors, coworkers, and more. When we listen to the news, we hear about crises of all kinds all over the world.

God calls missionaries to assist others across the globe, and we applaud those who have followed God's prompting. When we think about what the ultimate missionary looks like, we may also think about Mother Teresa, who gave up everything to help the poorest and most downtrodden. Or we might remember someone who traveled to build water wells, houses, and revitalize ravaged places into healthy lands. Or recall those aboard a floating hospital, helping victims of Ebola or some other disease that has had an impact across the world. Oftentimes, we think that overseas is the only missionary experience that exists.

However, one of the things we can admire about Paul (formerly Saul) is that he went to his own people, as well as those on foreign soil. Paul's transformation on the road to Damascus was so significant that he chose to sacrifice his own desires for the sake of sharing Jesus Christ with others (see Acts 9). He shared Christ with King Agrippa, a Roman official (Acts 26), but dedicated himself to share his life within his own culture (see Acts 23). He confronted others because of Christ, including a Jewish "sorcerer and false prophet named Bar-Jesus," who opposed his missionary work (Acts 13:6–11). Paul was the ultimate missionary!

We who follow Christ today can share God's love and grace with others and we can do it without necessarily crossing the waters. Paul's model is an inspiration for all of us to help others in need no matter where they are, and to share Jesus at all costs. We can't help but receive joy when we help others. God uses missionaries from other countries, which is awesome. But He can use us right where we are when we ask God to use us.

Dear Lord, please let me know how I can be a missionary right where I live, as well as to the rest of the world. I want to help make a difference in others' lives, and look forward to the joy that it will not only bring them, but me too. Thank You for hearing my prayer. Amen.

REFLECTION:
Look around. Where might your "mission field" be?

Suggested Scripture Reading: Acts 20:24;
2 Corinthians 5:18–21; 1 Peter 3:15

ROYALTY

RESNA MARIE BRUNSON

*But you are a chosen people, a royal priesthood,
a holy nation, God's special possession, that you
may declare the praises of him who called you
out of darkness into his wonderful light.*

1 PETER 2:9 NIV

Apple picking is one of our family's favorite activities. My husband and I began doing this when our children were very young and although we are now parents to two young adults and one teen, this fall activity continues to be something we all look forward to doing together. A highlight of the day would be to sit on Daddy's shoulder and pick an apple from the top of an apple tree. I used this experience as a teachable moment.

"You are God's possession," I told my daughters. "You are like the apples at the top of an apple tree. Those apples are bigger, brighter, and juicier. They are not touched or bruised by people who brush by the tree and they are closer to the sun. Unlike the lower apples, people have to work harder to get them. That is you," I told them.

My hope was for them to remember this when they started dating: that they are so very precious in God's eyes. They are not the apples that have been picked, consumed, and thrown to the ground; they are the ones one has to work to get.

How does the Word assure you of how precious you are to God?

You are chosen. Before conception, the all-sufficient God who made everything out of nothing purposely chose to create you in His image and according to His likeness (Genesis 1:27).

You are His special possession. For years I worked in adoptions and what a joy it was to unite a child with a "forever" family. As a Christian you belong to God's forever family. He will love and care for you, comfort you, and walk with you (Deuteronomy 7:6).

You are royalty! Many are fascinated by the life of royal families. Our fairy tales often depict the lives of kings, queens, princesses, and princes. But Christians need not look to characters. You are a member of God's royal family. Our God is the King and He owns the cattle on a thousand hills (Psalm 50:10). Once you become a Christian you are marked with a seal and guaranteed an inheritance.

It is biblical for parents to leave their children an inheritance. This does not solely need to be monetary. Parents can leave their children with a spiritual legacy—one with perfect assurance of their spiritual destiny. One with perfect assurance of their spiritual worth.

> *Father God, thank You for choosing me. Thank*
> *You for looking beyond my faults and accepting*
> *me into Your royal family. Forgive me for times*
> *I do not act worthy of my calling. I choose*
> *today to live as Your special possession.*

REFLECTION:
What spiritual legacy are you leaving your children?

Suggested Scripture Reading: Psalm 50:10;
Ephesians 1:13–15; 1 Peter 2:9

Passing the Baton

Diane Proctor Reeder

*Terah took his son Abram, his grandson Lot son
of Haran, and his daughter-in-law Sarai, the
wife of his son Abram, and together they set out
from Ur of the Chaldeans to go to Canaan. But
when they came to Harran, they settled there.*

Genesis 11:31

A re you a teacher?"
    I can't tell you how many times I have been asked
that question. Both my parents were in education, and both of
them thought education would be a great profession for me.

"You are such a teacher!"

I get that every time I present to a group. I am emphatically not a teacher. I am a writer, and I speak to groups about
what I write, and I am asked to lead Bible studies and Sunday school classes at my own church and at conferences.

But no matter how hard I try, I can't seem to get away
from the "teacher" moniker. I guess it's in my genes!

Spiritual genes, that is.

Our connection to our parents and our ancestry does not
dictate that we should automatically do what they do. But it
does inform the work that God has ordained for us. In other
words, we inherit more than just their DNA. We "inherit"
the values and principles that they hand down to us. And
sometimes, we inherit—and advance—the work that they do.

We must make the fine distinctions between passing down
a profession and passing down a life. After all, some parents
want their children to do exactly what they've done. Pastors

sometimes try to pass on the pastorate to their children. Corporate heads try to make their sons or daughters the "heir apparent." Sometimes those transitions are God-ordained, and sometimes they are not. It is not our place to be the final arbiter of those transitions. God has the final answer there.

We have a better way, an alternative to pigeonholing our children into doing what we do. We can instead share *why* we do what we do. We can give our children the gift of *intention*.

Father of the Hebrew patriarch Abraham, Terah had an interesting profession. He made idols that the surrounding nations then used in their worship ceremonies. But God called Abram to another "profession." God called Abram to do something his father had not done. But he also called Abram to the "original intent" of his father. Terah was, remember, headed for Canaan, the promised land that God would eventually carve out for Abraham and the Hebrew people (Genesis 11:31).

He called Abram, in other words, to the "original intent" of his father. Abraham, as he was now called, was destined to populate nations with his spiritual heritage as well as his DNA. We are the beneficiaries of that heritage today.

When we think about it, each of us has a personal spiritual heritage. Our spiritual journeys are peppered with God's intentions for us. Let's think prayerfully about how we can leave a spiritual legacy that includes not only what we did for God, but the deeper intentions of His heart—and ours.

REFLECTION:
What spiritual legacy did your parents, grandparents, or other ancestors share with you?

Suggested Scripture Reading: Psalm 145:4–5

Walk in the Good Way

Patricia Raybon

This is what the LORD says: "Stand at the cross-roads and look; ask for the ancient paths, ask where the good way is, and walk in it, and you will find rest for your souls."

JEREMIAH 6:16 NIV

A good parent can do us right. And bad parents? Their legacy can hurt an entire family, sending generations down a path into death if they follow ungodly ways. If that's your family legacy, can you ever redeem it? That was the choice, in the Bible, that faced the Sons of Korah. As descendants of the rebel Korah, their line arose from a man who rebelled against God—and paid a heavy price.

You may recall the story. During Moses's time, a man named Kohath, a son of Levi, was charged with carrying the holy things of the tabernacle, along with the other Kohathites—but on their shoulders. It was heavy, terrifying work—called on whenever the Israelites broke camp and moved. The tough part? The Kohathites couldn't actually touch the holy items or they would die. Only Levites could handle the items, wrapping them in special coverings before handing them off to Kohathites, who resented the task.

Rebelling, Kohath's grandson Korah rallied 250 leaders to challenge the rights of Moses and Aaron's priesthood as determined by God (Numbers 16). Such utter contempt for God's sovereignty resulted in Korah's horrifying death. He was buried alive. In a show of God's power, the earth opened its mouth and swallowed Korah and his fellow rebels "into the realm of the dead, with everything they owned." Then "the earth closed over them, and they perished and were gone from the community" (Numbers 16:33 NIV).

Several generations later, however, Korah's terrible legacy was transformed. The line of Korah came to include the great prophet Samuel, plus gatekeepers and custodians of the tabernacle (1 Chronicles 9:19–21), military warriors for David, and, in particular, great choral and orchestral music leaders (1 Chronicles 6:31–38). Sons of Korah are credited with writing 11 of the Bible's psalms, including Psalm 46 with its powering declaration: "God is our refuge and strength . . . Therefore we will not fear, though the earth give away and the mountains fall into the heart of the sea" (vv. 1–3). Who better to know that not even a quaking earth can undo God's ever-present help in times of trouble?

What a turnaround for this family. Humbled by their renewal in God, they wrote music that instructs: "Be still, and know that I am God . . . I will be exalted in the earth" (Psalm 46:10 NIV).

How did God redeem this broken family? They turned from sin, following God's commandments (Exodus 20:6)—choosing God's good way. In Christ today, we each can make this same good choice, and not wait for generations. Decide today for family healing, redeemed life, and—here's a bonus—"rest for our souls" (Jeremiah 6:16).

REFLECTION:
What negative family legacy will you allow the Lord to transform? How?

Suggested Scripture Reading: Numbers 16; Psalm 46

The Secret Place

Joyce Dinkins

He is my refuge and my fortress.

Psalm 91:2 NIV

Do you long to know your ancestors—who they were and how they endured? Piecing together their lives with fragments of stories and no photographs, or birth certificates, or known family name, or home place is puzzling. Each new piece of information—even that which reflects their struggles, can soothe the heart. Each "find" holds what's been secret, for so long thought lost completely.

My grandmother Bertha Marshall Powell shows up as a thirteen-year-old on the 1900 US Census of the Oklahoma Reservation, which lists her family as Creek Indian. Bertha's "identity" changed four times on later censuses, finally ending as Black on a state census roll. Later censuses record my grandmother living in Georgia and then Florida, where she and her children worked and gleaned fields. She'd had a husband, John, who had perished during WWI. What she was known for and is remembered for is how she cared for her children.

In tenant farm shacks, Bertha raised her and John's two children, but eventually three more of her own, including an orphan she took in whom her sister could no longer care for. Her name was Queenie. Bertha could barely read, if at all. Of the two photos atop my writing desk that frame her beautiful black face and strong hands—one is of her holding her adult son's arm, my uncle George. In the other, she's cradling a large Bible.

Just *holding* a Bible. Its treasures a secret to her mind in one way, yet known to her spirit in some other way. Bertha prayed for and took care of her children. Training them right beside her, Bertha harvested plenty. Her middle child, Lois, my mother, was the first of Bertha's two children by a local farmer. Mom's skin pigment brought her struggles. She appeared to be a child of her neighbor father, but he never accepted her. Others often excluded mom, asking "What is she?" because her skin looked so different from her mother's; they knew. Mom did not; she was a child.

The Lord moved my mother to attend church one day. As a teen, she attended a Black church and came forward to receive Jesus. She had some secret epiphany of light shining one night in her home around that time. A miracle is all she could explain it as because there was no electricity in their shack.

At high school graduation, she received a Bible. She was disappointed the church didn't give the students money to attend the historically Black college.

Because all she could then do was become a maid. Of course, she hid her hurts in her prayers as her mother had before her, and showed the hard work ethic that made her a sought-after servant, helping to provide for herself, her mother, and siblings. Her sister Queenie got a scholarship and Mom sent her help to go to college, and to study French in Paris. Imagine that! Who would have thought?

Leaning on prayer, Mom overcame "in the secret place of the Most High God" (Psalm 91:1). In her adulthood, on the coffee table inside her bedroom, Mom kept a booklet with praying hands illustrated on its cover. She did not talk so much about what she believed. Bowing on her knees by her bedside, lowering her head with a quiet prayer at meals, caring for us with all her might, helping the neighbor's children—quietly revealed her lifestyle, inside and outside church, which she attended only infrequently. Though she would dress and send us in handpicked, starched-and-pressed hand-me-downs. She said, "He is my refuge and my fortress" (Psalm 91:2), believed it, and He is. When she died at age 91, we could truly say "with long life God had satisfied" her and had given her "salvation" (paraphrase 91:16).

REFLECTION:
What did your ancestors overcome and how? What is the impact on you?

Suggested Scripture Reading: Psalm 91

Sister Hagar

Diane Proctor Reeder

*She gave this name to the LORD who spoke to her:
"You are the God who sees me," for she said, "I have
now seen the One who sees me."*

GENESIS 16:13 NIV

Poor Sister Hagar. An African woman, a child of Egypt, and a maidservant, or "slave," if you will. Her mistress, Sarai, "gave" her to Abram in order for him to father a child: "Go," she tells Abram, "sleep with my slave; perhaps I can build a family through her" (Genesis 16:2 NIV). And so Abram did.

And then, tension develops between the wife Sarai and the concubine-slave Hagar. It begins almost as soon as Hagar and Abram's son is conceived, and it continues even after Abram and Sarai's son, Isaac, is born. "When she [Hagar] knew she was pregnant, she began to despise her mistress" (Genesis 16:4 NIV).

Hagar flees from the abusive Sarai and finds herself in the desert. God promised her then that He would "increase your descendants so much that they will be too numerous to count" (Genesis 16:10 NIV). Hagar is amazed at this heavenly encounter, and we find in her response the first name for God ever recorded: El Roi, "The God who sees me" (Genesis 16:13 NIV).

I find myself identifying our African-American people with Hagar. Our ancestors were similarly acted upon by people interested only in exploitation. We also had no say in the matter of our bodies and to whom we bore our children. Then, we were sent on our way to an unknown future, with even less than Hagar received from her masters.

Later, God speaks to Hagar again when she once again finds herself in the desert after being evicted by Abram and Sarai.

> *"What is the matter, Hagar? Do not be afraid;*
> *God has heard the boy crying as he lies there. Lift*
> *the boy up and take him by the hand, for I will*
> *make him into a great nation."*
> (GENESIS 21:17–18 NIV).

God saw this maidservant, concubine-slave. He made promises to her. He revealed Himself to this African woman. Centuries later, He would reveal Himself to our ancestors, and we would, amazed, respond with our own names for God based on our special encounter with Him. He was the "Waymaker." The "Burden-Bearer." The "Heavy Load Sharer." Just as He did with Hagar, God makes Himself known to those who struggle, to those who call on His name in the depths of their circumstances.

Thank you, Hagar, for paving the way. For letting us know that we serve a God who is intimately engaged with our suffering. For reminding us that He can make a "Way out of No Way."

REFLECTION:
What similarities can you find between Hagar, the Israelites, and the African-American enslavement experience? What do those similarites teach us about the character of God?

Suggested Scripture Reading: Genesis 16; 21

GOD OPENED ANOTHER DOOR

MARVIN A. McMICKLE

God has given us different gifts for doing certain things well.

ROMANS 12:6

The African-American church has emerged as one of the most vibrant locations of praise and worship to be found anywhere in the world. This rich heritage of worship began during slavery in "hush harbors"—isolated, secret locations where slaves would gather at night for hours of prayer and singing without fear of being heard. Those gatherings gave birth to the "Negro spirituals" that wedded together their sorrows and their faith into lyrics like "Nobody knows de trouble I've seen . . . Glory, hallelujah."

Other musical forms and gifted singers have also come from the African-American church. And the power and rhythm of African-American preaching is well regarded. Beginning with slave preachers, African-American preachers have ministered to the needs of the brokenhearted, to the sins of a broken nation, and to leaders and other people all over the world. And their churches have become central cultural institutions for education, training, and other human services, as well as for civil rights activism.

These churches also launched African-American missionaries serving in the United States and the world. John Marrant served the American Indian People. George Liele headed to the Caribbean. David George served in Nova Scotia and planted the first Baptist church for Blacks in Silver Bluff, North Carolina. Prince Williams planted churches in the Bahamas. Former slave Lott Carey became America's first missionary to Africa. William Henry Shepherd went to the heart of the Congo to preach, provide medical aid, and more. And a growing number of independent churches and denominations performed missions at home to congregants soaring into the tens of millions of African Americans.

African-American Christian educators Nannie Helen Burroughs, Mary McLeod Bethune, William Augustus Jones, Kelly Miller, and many others served to establish educational institutions, including the dozens of historically Black colleges and universities begun by Christians.

From Christian folk artists, to celebrated visionaries, African-American contributions have helped and continue to help beautify the world. James Weldon Johnson's classic poem, "The Creation," and his song, "Lift Ev'ry Voice and Sing" (The Negro National Anthem) prevail across denominations. Biblical artist Henry Ossawa Tanner ("The Banjo Maker"; "The Thankful Poor"; "Daniel in the Lion's Den"; "Jesus Visiting Nicodemus") is celebrated the world over. If a door closed at one venue, God opened another.

God has provided a diversity of gifts for service in the church, all significant when used in His Spirit of love for Him and humanity (1 Corinthians 12:27–13:1). That's a legacy.

God has given gifts for service.

REFLECTION:
God's gracious gifts are evident in the African-American church historically. What gifts do you see in your church?

Suggested Scripture Reading: 1 Corinthians 12:1–14; 13:1

The Practice of Remembering

A. C. Cobbs

He took some bread and gave thanks to God for it. Then he broke it in pieces and gave it to the disciples, saying, "This is my body, which is given for you. Do this in remembrance of me."

Luke 22:19

The name *Leon Smith* is not a household name, yet his life is associated with history. On September 11, 2001, three hundred forty-three firefighters lost their lives responding to the terrorist attack on the World Trade Center. Among the number were twelve African-American firefighters. Leon Smith, part of Ladder Company 118, was one of the brave men who died that day. His body was never recovered. The heroic acts of these twelve men seemed destined to be overlooked like many people of color before them. The mothers of these men, however, are determined to make sure their sons are not forgotten and the world knows not only who they were but also the sacrifice they made.

The night before His death, Jesus sat in a secluded upper room eating dinner with His disciples. The mood of the night was somber as He took a piece of bread and told them, "This is my body which is given for you; do this in remembrance of me" (Luke 22:19). Jesus used the meal to inform His friends of His assignment to lay down His life for the forgiveness of sins. He then gave them an assignment of their own; to remember the sacrifice He made. By this, Jesus introduced the practice of remembering the brutal death He endured on our behalf. Paul later elaborated on the purpose, "For whenever you eat this bread and drink this cup, you proclaim the Lord's death until he comes" (1 Corinthians 11:26 NIV). Believers who commemorate Jesus's death are not only reminded of the act but also relay the story to others.

Jesus understood how easy it is for people to forget the sacrifices others have made throughout history. When there is no intentional gesture or way to commemorate, memories fade. But when a life is remembered, a story is told.

Lord, thank You for those who have sacrificed
for our freedom, safety, and well-being.
Thank You most of all for Jesus who
died that we might live.

REFLECTION:
How do you remember those who have sacrificed for you? Remembering them ensures that their stories live on.

Suggested Scripture Reading: 1 Corinthians 11:23

When We Pray

Marvin Williams

But Jesus often withdrew to lonely places and prayed.

LUKE 5:16 NIV

When I was growing up, I was in awe when I listened to my mother and other mothers in our church pray. Sometimes they would sit in silence and whisper words to the Father. Still other times, they would lay themselves down prostrate and weep prayers to God. I watched these saints raise their hands and stretch out their arms as they sang that familiar hymn by Dr. Watts:

> Father, I stretch my hands to Thee.
> No other help I know.
> If Thou withdraw Thy help from me,
> oh, whither shall I go?

I remember the way the room seemed to shake with divine power. Though I couldn't see Him, I could feel God's power when these saints worshiped in prayer. I know from my childhood that prayer can be joyful and life-changing. And some days it is. But there are other days when it feels mundane and monotonous. Yet the legacy of faith I experienced lives in me. I still long to hear the Father tell me who He is, who I am, and where I am going. I still long to experience in prayer the joy only He can give.

And when I reflect on some of the reasons we pray, I'm motivated to keep pressing on. As His beloved children in

Christ (Ephesians 5:1), through the Spirit we cry out to God as our Father, our Abba (Galatians 4:6). When we turn to Him, He has compassion on us, knowing how vulnerable we are (Psalm 103:13–14). Like a good father, through His grace, God gives us what we do not deserve, while mercifully shielding us from what we deserve (Romans 8:15; Galatians 4:6). Prayer nurtures this tender relationship with our Father.

When my oldest son was diagnosed with a condition best known as "lazy eye," the doctor said that his vision in one eye was reduced, and he would eventually go blind in that eye. My wife and I called the prayer team at our church, and they gathered around my son and prayed for him. We prayed because God invited us to draw near to the throne of grace that we might receive mercy and find grace in time of need (Hebrews 4:16). We prayed, cried, and trusted. We prayed because God invites us to pray, and when we do, our Father responds to the cries of His children—in the time and in the ways that are best. And in our moment of desperate need, we experienced His power and love and supernatural healing.

The older I get, the more I realize why the prayers of the saints of old in the Black church were so powerful and effective. They didn't just know about God; they knew God personally. The *why* of their prayers preceded the *what* of their prayers. They prayed, not out of duty, but from their desperate need for His presence and power. They prayed not to get stuff from God, but to get God.

REFLECTION:
What is a fresh testimony you can share about God and you?

Suggested Scripture Reading: Matthew 6:1–14

Built on the Solid Rock

Tondra L. Loder-Jackson

*And I say also unto thee, that thou art Peter, and
upon this rock I will build my church; and the gates
of hell shall not prevail against it.*

Matthew 16:18 KJV

"I am struggling with my church."

I have heard and expressed this lament quite often on
my long Christian journey, typically in the aftermath of a
bitter church split, a high-profile scandal, or burnout from
giving so much and receiving so little. I have been a member
of predominantly Black churches all of my life. Although not
unique among churches in the United States for their short-
comings, Black churches more often than not are fodder for
jokes and nighttime soap operas. Black preachers are paro-
died as shady, verbose, and prosperity-seeking men leading
compliant (mostly women) parishioners titillated by enter-
tainment over substance.

The Pew Research Center notes that African Americans
stand out as the most religiously committed racial/ethnic
group in the nation. African Americans attend religious services, pray daily, and espouse an unwavering belief in God at
higher rates than other Americans. Indeed, the Black church
has stood the test of time and faith from enslavement to freedom in spite of its heightened scrutiny.

Similar to Jesus's disciple Peter, "the Black church," as it is
so often referred monolithically, is fraught with human frailty
yet striving to get right with God. Peter vacillated between
being sold out for Jesus to denying that he ever knew him in

His darkest hour (John 18:15–27). Yet Jesus restored Peter into a right relationship with Him (John 21:15–17), proclaiming him a Rock on which the Christian church would stand for ages to come. He ultimately became one of the most fiery and boldest among Jesus's apostles.

What will be the enduring legacy of the Black church for successive generations? Do younger generations know the true history of the Black church's perseverance and faithfulness to Christ through trials and tribulations? How will they build on this rock-solid foundation?

REFLECTION:

> "On Christ, the solid Rock, I stand;
> All other ground is sinking sand,
> All other ground is sinking sand."
> —EDWARD MOTE (1797–1874)

Suggested Scripture Reading: Judges 2:6–15; Joel 1:3

His Hold

Joyce Dinkins

One generation commends your works to another; they tell of your mighty acts.

PSALM 145:4 NIV

Gazing at blue skies while sprawled across the warm sidewalk in front of our comfortable home in suburban Chicago, my young mind strained to comprehend the stories of racial obstacles our parents recounted. But our upbringing in the 1950s meant we in particular would be told in intimate, relevant detail about the centuries of oppression, loss, and pain our forbears experienced and how that continued to permeate our parents' lives and touched our futures.

Although they taught us how to be strong, their lives provoked trust *beyond* their own strength—faith in God's power. God had planted in them an overcoming mindset that had at its center what I recognize as hope in *Him*. I celebrate this hope that my ancestors knew. After all these centuries and all that has transpired, He remains our Help, able to inspire generations today. The Bible declares this fact and encouragement to us, "In this world you will have trouble. But take heart! I have overcome the world" (John 16:33 NIV).

When his granddaughter was completing a Black History Month assignment, my father taught her, "Slavery really hurt your great-grandfather because he had such free desires. My dad was owned, like a pair of shoes someone gets up in the morning to put on." Detailing slavery's legacies and counseling her about prejudices she was already facing in the 1990s, my dad traced what he could about his grandparents: "From

Africa, they were likely brought in on slave ships through the Carolinas, and then sold." And then Dad encouraged her about Africa also being the cradle of humanity, a forerunner of civilization, wealthy with kingdoms and cultural accomplishments.

And based on his dad's teaching, my father, "W. A." as people called him, handed down to our family the Golden Rule. He reminded us about doing to others what you would have them do to you (see Luke 6:31). However, he had mixed emotions about what others had done to *him* and *his* family, including some churches and preachers who had twisted God's truth to preserve brutal slavery. But he also warned against prejudice, insisting, "Treat people as individuals." And he talked about faithful Christian believers he knew who had pressed for abolition and justice and given us hope. People like some Quaker families, including one that reached out, helping Dad get housing and medical care, doing as Jesus taught His followers to do (Matthew 22:37–40). Dad then reemphasized education and hard work.

The historic Black church had provided nurture for Dad. Dad complained about the mule wagon rides to church Sundays for all-day services, but praised his schooling there from somewhere around 1911 to 1915. At the smell of rain, cotton picking would stop, rescuing W. A. from backbreaking labor. Then school began in a one-room Black church his great uncle and other former slaves had helped plant. His father, Millard, would keep the fireplaces warming the church. And aunts who attended historic Spelman Seminary taught with The Blue Back Speller focusing on literacy and Christ. These teachers challenged the younger and older sharecroppers to excel, believing education equaled escape from poverty. But they always counted on Christ to help them overcome, and held on to His unchanging hand.

REFLECTION:
What are ways that you can see God has upheld your family throughout the generations?

Suggested Scripture Reading: Psalm 145

Just a Dash—A Dash
Between Two Dates

Otis Moss Jr.

*Teach us to number our days, that we may gain
a heart of wisdom.*

PSALM 90:12 NIV

There is a great prayer in the book of Psalms that we know well. Although we may not always treat it as a prayer. It is used more often at funerals than at births. And perhaps that is a misplaced emphasis, although it's appropriate in both places. It's relevant at birth, consecrations, and dedications. The twelfth verse of Psalm 90 simply says: "So teach us to number our days, that we may apply our hearts unto wisdom (KJV). Another translation reads, "Teach us to count our days that we may gain a wise heart" (NRSV).

This prayer is saying: God, teach us to make the proper use of the time we are given that our hearts might be right for mission and purpose. Lord, teach us to appreciate every moment, every day, every hour that we may apply all of our powers to do that which is right.

Think about it in this way: we're living and serving on a dash between two dates. Now, in your mind, take out a pencil and write down the year of your birth. And then draw a little dash. And at the end of that short line, write a question mark. And allow that to be a kind of pushing, haunting reminder of the fact that we all live on a little dash between two dates.

Two of my elders, one a special mentor, awakened this in my consciousness more than fifty years ago. They were not aware of that because they were not dealing specifically with this Scripture text or even extensively with the idea. One of the elders was my college president, Benjamin Elijah Mays, who taught us that it's not how long you live but how well you live. He was Dr. Martin Luther King Jr.'s friend and mentor. The other was the late Dr. Vernon Johns, who was King's predecessor, at Dexter Avenue Baptist Church, Montgomery, Alabama. Johns was giving a commencement address more than 50 years ago at a gathering of Atlanta University, Morehouse College, and Spelman College. He gave the baccalaureate address. He referenced "the dash" as our life's journey. Johns said you ought to do at least three things with life: "enlarge it, immortalize it, and trust its mystery," and in the course of unfolding this, he almost casually mentioned the little dash between two dates. That dash is what God has given to us. It's just a moment.

You know when you are ten years old, 20 years sounds like a long time, but when you're 21, it was just a fleeting moment. When you are 20, 50 may sound like a millennium, but when you are 51, it was just a flash! Quicker than hello and sooner than goodbye. Just a dash between two dates. And there is, and there should be, that haunting question, what am I doing? What can I do? What should I do on that little dash? Whether the dash is but a dot or whether it's a moment that takes us into senior years, the responsibility is to do good on the dash. Whether you are young or whether you are mature in years.

God has given to each of us on that dash three things: a gift, an opportunity, a responsibility. The gift that God has placed in our hands. An opportunity to say yes to God and to give our best in return. And it's also a responsibility that we must give an account of. You know, the dash is that calling from God to learn, to climb, and to serve.

I know a doctor who heads up one of the greatest medical institutions in the world. He was turned down by a dozen medical schools before he could become a doctor. He had to overcome a challenge. But one day, the doctor said to me he had performed 22,000 heart surgeries. . . . On a dash between two dates. When 12 medical colleges had said no, finally one said yes. In spite of his challenge, his dyslexia, God put the tools in his hands, the genius in his mind, and folk are walking around right now breathing and serving because he performed open-heart surgery and gave them a new lease on life.

The keynote speaker at Gettysburg Cemetery during the Civil War was a gifted orator from Harvard. He spoke two hours. Lincoln's name was not even on the program; he was simply listed as "remarks from the president." Nobody remembers the keynote speaker's name or anything he said. Lincoln spoke two minutes and everyone remembers all of his words—The Gettysburg Address!

You don't have to live long to do God's work. Just live well according to the will and way and calling of God. We must know that life itself is a dash between two dates. So the critical question we have to raise with ourselves is: what must I do with my dash?

Here is how some have used the dash between their two dates. . . . When I was a young pastor in my early twenties, I went to the hospital to visit a nine-year-old child who was suffering cancer. He had only been recently baptized by my hands. But I noticed something special in the youngster's hospital room on the little table beside the bed—a stack of books, pencil, pen, and paper. I asked, "What are you doing with these books?" He said, "Reverend Moss, I don't want to get behind in my schoolwork." In less than 6 months, this child was dead but he had not given up making full use of the little dash between two dates, from birth to nine years old. He didn't spend that time moaning and groaning and complaining and arguing with God. He continued to do his schoolwork.

I believe God is saying to each of us, whatever time you have, spend your time wisely. Do your homework well. Do your community service well. Do your mission assignment as though, to quote another, "God sent you into the world for the express purpose of doing this job."

If you want further proof, talk about Wilma Rudolph. On her dash there was scarlet fever. On her dash was polio. On her dash was double pneumonia. But God still put running in her legs. And with a coach at Tennessee State University, she stood tall, stood out, and performed well. In 1960, after the Olympics in Rome, she brought home three gold and one bronze medal. She died years later from brain cancer, but on her dash, her grandmother wouldn't stop praying for her and she wouldn't stop responding to grandma's prayers and the grace of God. So she went to her grave with those medals and made history on a little dash.

Dr. Mordecai Johnson had a one-semester suspension from Morehouse. He had such genius and dedication that he didn't want his parents to know that he had been suspended for a minor infraction, so he went from Atlanta to Chicago and got a job. His roommate would receive his letters from home and mail the letters in Atlanta so they would have the Atlanta postmark! He was in Chicago and his parents thought he was in Atlanta. You could do that in those days before the Internet and smartphones. When his one semester suspension was up, he came back and doubled the load, and graduated on time, as valedictorian. Then one day when he was a pastor of a church in West Virginia, Howard University offered him its presidency. Some of the most influential persons in America told him don't take it. They said he would be the first African-American president of Howard University and that the school was in chaos and deep debt. They warned Mordecai, "Stay where you are."

Mordecai Johnson believed God would guide him through the presidency of this school. When he went to Howard, the law school was unaccredited. It was a night school. He raised it to accreditation. The divinity school was unaccredited. He raised it to accreditation too. And under the tutelage of Charles Hamilton Houston, a young student named Thurgood Marshall graduated from Howard University School of Law.

In 1935, Thurgood Marshall and Charles Hamilton Houston and others sat down and mapped out a strategy to break up the racial apartheid system that held its grip on the South for decades following Emancipation. They said it would take 20 years to get rid of the system of laws that segregated and disenfranchised and enforced a system of "Whites Only" and "Colored Only" barriers on all of life. By the 19th year, the Supreme Court decision was handed down to end "Jim Crow" segregation.

Thurgood Marshall went to the Supreme Court 32 times and won 29 times. Even though the University of Maryland had turned him down. But God fixed it. So Thurgood Marshall, who was turned down by the University of Maryland would carry a case to the Supreme Court against the University of Maryland that had turned him down and closed the doors in his face. Now when you go to Baltimore, Maryland, the airport is Thurgood Marshall Airport. You can't take off and you can't land without saying Thurgood's name. All this on just a dash. "So teach us to number our days that we may apply our hearts unto wisdom."

Over 100 years ago Benjamin Elijah Mays was praying and plowing a mule somewhere outside of Epworth, South Carolina. Dr. Mays didn't graduate from high school until he was 21—not because he was slow in learning but in those days Black youth could only go to school three or four months out of the year. Sometimes plowing with a mule, he would stop at the end of the row and tie the mule and get down on his knees and pray to God for an education! His mother nor father could read or write. But he entered Bates College and graduated Phi Beta Kappa. On a dash between two dates!

I might tell you about a young girl named Anne Frank and a young man named Martin Luther King Jr. Both were born in 1929, one on this side and the other on the other side of the Atlantic. Anne Frank died in a Nazi concentration camp before her sixteenth birthday. Martin Luther King Jr. entered Morehouse before age 16. Both made wise use of their little dash. Anne Frank wrote a diary that was almost destroyed in a trash pile but sold more than 30 million copies in 67 languages. And before Dr. Martin Luther King could reach his fortieth birthday, he was killed by an assassin's bullet of hate. But before he died, he opened doors that some people are walking through right now and don't know who opened the door. But on that dash, he did God's will so well that even his enemies now quote his words. Just a dash between two dates.

And you know, one day we've got to turn in our dash. We must be careful how we handle our dash. I cannot entrust my dash to just anybody and neither can you. My dash belongs to the One who gave it to me. "From everlasting to everlasting, thou art God" (Psalm 90:2). My dash, our dash, belongs to who is "from everlasting to everlasting." God is. The Lord is. God is never a past-tense God. God is. Alexander the Great was but God is. God is the strength of my life. God never fails. I'm failing everyday but God is the strength of my life. Jesus—more powerful on a donkey, and in a grave, than Caesar was in a palace! Jesus is the Light of the World and with Jesus my dash is in eternal hands. Thank You, Jesus. Thanks be to God for a little dash between two dates! Amen.

GRANDMA'S INFLUENCE

SHARON NORRIS ELLIOTT

After the wind blows, the flower is gone, and there is no sign of where it was. But the LORD's love for those who respect him continues forever and ever, and his goodness continues to their grandchildren.

PSALM 103:16–17 NCV

As grandparents go, I only knew my maternal grand-mother. Born in the 1880s, Mary Francis Magdelene Wormly Delacy Jennings was an extremely fair-skinned African-American woman who had seven pregnancies, suffered through four still-births, and mourned the deaths of two husbands. My dad packed her up as well when he decided to move my mom (her only daughter) and two of her grand-kids (my brother and sister) all the way across the country from Maryland to California. She was the quiet presence who listened to The Biola Hour radio program in her room, ironed sheets, and made our beds. She would let Cissi (my best friend) and me comb her completely white hair into all kinds of styles that looked amazing to us.

The manner in which Grandma influenced my life the most was in the area of music. When she recognized I would pick out little melodies rather than just bang on the piano keys, she started paying for me to take piano lessons. Starting when I was five years old, I took eleven years of classical piano lessons, starting with John Thompson's *Teaching Little Fingers to Play* and progressing all the way to playing the classical masterpieces of Bach, Beethoven, Chopin, and others.

Grandma sat through every 30-minute daily practice as if she were in a box seat at Carnegie Hall until she moved into the swanky senior citizens' complex our church built. And oh my, my annual piano recitals might as well have been a command performance at the Disney Concert Hall in Los Angeles or at Australia's Opera House.

The only other things I know about my grandmother are her partial Native-American background, her inability to fully use one of her arms, the fact that she had sisters who lived in a fourth floor walk-up in a Harlem, New York tenement, and the fact that despite her intelligence, she was only allowed to receive a fifth-grade education. I knew she loved me, and hers was the first funeral of a family member I ever attended. I was twelve.

I wish I had known more about my grandmother. Knowing about her life wasn't important to me then, but my ancestral background is very important to me now that I'm a grandmother myself. My grandbabies call me "Nana." I not only want to know my own roots, but I desire for my grandchildren to not just know about me, but to actually *know* me, feel what I was all about, and be proud of the legacy I'm leaving for them. Whenever I play the piano, I can recall all the enjoyable hours I've spent at the keyboard, and know that it was my sweet grandmother who gave that legacy to me.

I'm working on the legacy I'll leave for my precious grandchildren. As an author, of course, I love books. I have already started sharing books with my first grandson, Dallas. It looks like Nana, Dallas, and books will go together like Grandma, Sharon, and the piano did when I was a little girl. Dallas has wrapped his Nana around his little finger by loving books as much as I do. After one visit, my daughter-in-law told me that no one else could read those books with him because he had dubbed them to be "Nana books." To him, those were books only he and I would share.

Several of the books Dallas and I read together have Christian themes. Those books are a special sub-section of "Nana books" that he calls "God books." As much as I want him to know, remember, and love me, I want him to know, remember, and love God even more. Scripture backs me up in this desire. Psalm 145:3–4 says, "Great is the LORD! He is most worthy of praise! No one can measure his greatness. Let each generation tell its children of your mighty acts; let them proclaim your power." And Psalm 103:16–17 says, "After the wind blows, the flower is gone, and there is no sign of where it was. But the LORD's love for those who respect him continues forever and ever, and his goodness continues to their grand-children" (NCV).

When I first held each grandbaby in the delivery room, the first thing they heard Nana say in their little, newborn ears was "Jesus loves you." As I continue to learn how to play my Nana role, between the cuddles and kisses, I'm deliberately conscious of the godly legacy I want Dallas and his little sister Jordyn to realize. (This goes for any other future grandbabies that may come my way!) Proverbs 13:22 sums this idea up for us. "A good man leaves an inheritance to his children's children" (ESV). The Hebrew translation of "leaves an inheritance" is the word *nachal*. This word is used to mean posses-sions and land, just like we expect; however, the same idea is repeated in other areas of Scripture and it pertains to the testimony and wisdom we leave behind.

I'm grateful for my grandmother, her parents, and their parents, etc. No matter what the circumstances were, only the exact pairings in each generation could have led to the person I became. For all of us, whether it was bad or good, the past led up to the present in which we stand, and because of God's grace, we can move into a future of favor in His sight—a future that will allow us to leave a godly legacy for our grandchildren. So start piano lessons, read books, or share with those adorable grandbabies whatever it is God has gifted to you in your life. Leave an inheritance to your children's children.

REFLECTION:
What is it that your grandchildren will learn from you that they'll take into their future and tell their children about? Will they carry a positive testimony?

Suggested Scripture Reading: Psalms 103, 145; Proverbs 13

Who Will Be a Witness for My Lord?

Marvin A. McMickle

But you will receive power when the Holy Spirit comes upon you. And you will be my witnesses, telling people about me everywhere—in Jerusalem, throughout Judea, in Samaria, and to the ends of the earth.

Acts 1:8

Acts 1:6–8 includes a conversation between Jesus and His disciples before He ascended into heaven. Jesus voiced this final challenge: "Be my witnesses in Jerusalem, and in all Judea and Samaria, and to the ends of the earth" (1:8 NIV). I suggest that the church today embrace this challenge as its own. Jesus has the same interest today in spreading His message as widely as possible as He did when these words were first spoken.

Jerusalem is the local community in which each of us lives, and includes the problems and the people who are just around the corner or right down the street. Judea refers to our nation and to the broader social and cultural issues that have an impact on people across the country. Samaria reminds us to carry our message and show love to the people society may have urged us to scorn or avoid due to racial, language, religious, criminal background, or even lifestyle issues. Going to the ends of the earth is a reminder that the God who created the world has a global concern, and is not limited only to what happens in any one country.

Acts 1:6–8 is a challenge to every Christian to find a field of service where he or she can let his or her light of love and mercy shine. All of us cannot and need not travel to the ends of the earth; however, we can volunteer at a hunger center in our community. We can speak up for our values on issues like voting rights, affordable and accessible health care, or the human and financial costs of war. We can visit a prison or local jail to lead a Bible study or share in a church-sponsored worship service. Jesus reminds us in this passage that there is an available field of Christian service for anyone who wants to be a witness for the Lord.

There may be a deeper meaning for this passage, not so much where we choose to go and serve but what it means to be a witness for the Lord. There are three distinct ways by which every Christian can understand and model what it means to be a witness for the Lord.

The first is the simple idea of a witness as someone who has observed what was going on around him. Ezekiel 3:15 reminds us that the prophet sat for seven days among the people living in exile in Babylon before he uttered a word. Like Ezekiel, we could avoid saying anything to others about what God may have to say until after we have taken time to notice what is going on in their lives. We Christians need to pay attention to what is going on around us. We cannot live as if only our own circumstances matter. As witnesses for the Lord, we could begin by observing the needs of the people around us.

The second aspect of being a witness borrows from a courtroom setting where a witness swears an oath "to tell the truth, the whole truth, and nothing but the truth." Likewise, Christians should be prepared "to tell the truth, the whole truth, and nothing but the truth" about what they see going on in the world. In the face of human suffering, in response to unspeakable acts of human cruelty, in defense of the rights of the weakest and most vulnerable people in our society, Christians could speak truth as willing witnesses for the Lord.

It should be noted that there is a risk in going from observing to saying something. What we observe is a private matter. We may ponder what we have seen, but unless we say something about it, we do not reveal anything about our values or our view on the issue at hand. Many people are reluctant to speak up about injustice or matters of public policy. We may have strong personal opinions, but we may need the courage of our convictions sufficient to cause us to speak our mind, or better yet, to speak truth that reveals a godly way of thinking about what we have observed. It is safe to say that when Jesus called His disciples to be His witnesses, He called them to say something about what they had seen.

There is a reason why some people may be reluctant to speak openly about events going on in the world. This reluctance might have something to do with the Greek word for witness, which is *marturia*, a word that means "martyr." In Acts 1:8, Jesus essentially told His disciples to "be my martyrs." While He may not have been directing them to seek out death as a requirement for their discipleship, He was signaling to them that they could expect opposition and suffering as a consequence of what they would say in His name.

Many people refuse to speak up, because they are not willing or prepared to suffer as a consequence of being a witness. They do not mind going to church, paying their tithes, and volunteering every now and then. But they do not want to alienate friends, upset people in leadership, go against the grain of social custom, or risk career advancement because of taking an unpopular position on a controversial issue.

Consider these words from Jesus: "Whoever wants to save their life will lose it, but whoever loses their life for me will save it" (Luke 9:24). With that in mind, who will be a witness for my Lord?

God's Timing Is Perfect

Sheila Bailey

Stir up the gift of God which is in you.
2 Timothy 1:6 NKJV

It was my first plane ride, first time to the Southwest, and first time attending a school that was historically African-American as I entered Bishop College. The course of events God had planned for me over the following years during and after college graduation would mature me as a wife, mother, servant-leader, grandmother, and now widow.

Since Bishop was a religious college, all students were required to enroll in two semesters of religion courses. As I conversed with Christian Education professors I inquired, "Can you declare it as your major? Can you get a job in Christian Education? Will a church hire you, even an African-American church?" Their affirmative answers led to a greater interest as God was tugging at my heart to change my major from Business Administration to Christian Education.

As I approached graduation I prayed about job opportunities. I was excited about where God was going to send me. Of course, I would be involved in the teaching ministry of a church to organize programs for children, youth and adult ministries so "that all persons can be aware of God through Jesus Christ; grow as sons and daughters of God rooted in a Christian community with hope until Jesus's return." However, E. K. Bailey, my boyfriend, told me "most African-American churches do not have nor are hiring persons in the field of Christian Education." Those words were followed with the statement "Trust God!"

After graduation I began my search for a job in Christian Education, to no avail. E. K. Bailey and I were engaged. We had planned the wedding date. I continued to pray, "Lord, I need a job. Please give me the desire of my heart. I know you impressed on my heart Christian Education. I made good grades at Bishop. I'm serving you. Pretty please, God, a job in Christian Education."

It was as if the Omnipotent One looked over the balcony of heaven and said "Sheila, not now!"

When I was about at my wit's end looking for employment, I learned about the Baptist General Convention of Texas. They had an opening for me as a secretary in the Direct Missions Department. There, I began to learn the structure of a Southern Baptist State Convention in contrast to the predominantly African-American National Baptist Convention. There is richness in the legacy of both.

After a few months E. K. and I were married and moved to Fort Worth so he could attend Southwestern Baptist Theological Seminary. My search began for another job. I became a secretary once again, working for the Tarrant County Community Action Center.

Five months later the Mt. Carmel Baptist Church in Dallas extended the call for E. K. to be the pastor. Hallelujah! His prayer to pastor a church was answered. "So Lord, is this where you want me to serve too?" I prayed. God's answer: This wasn't the church where I would be in leadership as a Christian educator. So the search for another job began once again. I became a secretary to the president of the Interdenominational Ministers' Alliance, who was also a prominent pastor. My office was located in the apartment complex the church owned. There I served until I became secretary at my alma mater, Bishop College, in the admissions office, until our first child was born.

Women leaders at Mt. Carmel, as well as in the North Texas Baptist District Association, the Missionary Baptist General Convention of Texas, and the National Baptist Convention of America, began to recommend me to speak on programs. One door of opportunity led to another. God began to give me peace that the teaching ministry of the church takes place everywhere.

In 1975, after spending time in prayer, Concord Baptist Church was organized, and my husband, the founder, pastored there. People heard the vision for evangelism, discipleship, community outreach, and staff development, and joined the church. Shortly after moving into a church building, the leaders approached my husband and inquired if I had a degree in Christian Education—and they asked if I could become the Director of Christian Education. I was ecstatic! God was right on time!

I served a total of nine years. It was exhilarating beginning the teacher training program and organizing a Christian Education team of leaders committed to fulfilling the Great Commission (Matthew 28:19–20). But, to better serve my family at home, I resigned after a few years, and passed the baton to a successor. Can you believe I was asked to return as an interim Christian Education Director a few years later? Life is unpredictable. Lord, help me to understand your timing!

Have you been in God's waiting room? We can feel many emotions there. Discouragement, disappointment, anger, resentment, fatigue, and uncertainty can absorb our days. Often changes in life are sudden and unexpected. Up, down, and around, like a roller coaster ride. But God is always faithful! Allow me to share with you His helps:

The beauty of a consistent prayer life is its focus on the attributes of God. He is all-powerful and all knowing, protecting, and providing. We can agree with God when we miss the mark with our attitude or actions, confess pride, and ask for humility. Thank Him for all of His blessings without letting the blessings of others eclipse our view of God blessing each of us.

Assessing what needs to be cultivated in your life. One of the many lessons I had to learn was how to deal with difficult people, and about communicating with difficult temperaments. God was my Help.

Learning from others. A stellar administrator in the public school system assisted me in the Christian Education ministry. I learned many invaluable lessons from him, including that having authority doesn't mean you neglect the thoughts of others. Strive for goal sharing. Then it will be a joint decision everyone can value. I learned how to cast vision and share vision and build team relationships. God sends His help.

God uses our past to prepare us for our future. There is an old saying that my mother said, "Don't burn bridges that you may have to cross again." Each job was a building block for the next opportunity where God was leading me. I gained resources for ministry, met clergy leaders of all denominations, and developed lasting friendships as I organized and networked with leaders and members of their congregations. Having one office located at a government-supplemented apartment complex increased my sensitivity for the dynamics and needs of single-parent families and disenfranchised families. I accepted a supervisor that was totally an opposite personality and gained his respect, being mindful that we are in the world but not of the world. I learned how to strive for excellence in production and customer service while learning the unspoken politics of an institution. I needed all these lessons. I made many mistakes. But, God allowed those experiences so I did not err more.

Just be FAT. Faithful. Available. Teachable. He has surprises for us. I haven't been a Christian Education Director for many years but I'm continuously engaged in Christian education. Wherever Christ is shared in word or deed, Christian Education is taking place. It may be with my offspring, their children, grandchildren, a neighbor, or a stranger I meet. My title is no longer important. What matters is that I'm serving in Jesus's name, to help heal hurting humanity.

Don't limit God! Dream. A few years ago I was afraid to learn the computer. Shellguin Murray, a friend who is the right arm of Sheila B. Ministries, empowered me to overcome my fears. She showed me one step at a time how to begin to use my desktop. I used her directions, creating my own personal manual. Now I find God-directed surprises when online. There will be invitations to teach in cities throughout the US, and in the Caribbean, to church groups, colleges, and seminaries of different denominations and cultures. God is faithful to equip us. What He starts He is faithful to finish.

Be in a state of preparation. Pray, study, love God and all people, serve with gladness, persevere by faith! Discover and develop relationships with mentors and positive peers. "Stir up the gift of God which is in you" (2 Timothy 1:6 NKJV).

Seek and accept God's will. In the Greek wording, *kronos* refers to the time on the calendar or in the smartphone. But *kairos* means the providential time or the right time when God had scheduled it in eternity. According to my timetable, the position as Director of Christian Education had been delayed. According to God's timetable, He was on time. Our Help always is. His timing is perfect (Ecclesiastes 3:11).

GOD'S DREAM

WINTLEY PHIPPS

*"I knew you before I formed you in your
mother's womb.
   Before you were born I set you apart
   and appointed you as my prophet to the nations."*

JEREMIAH 1:5

I want to tell you something very important," my aunt said. She came by to see me not very long ago and after walking around my home looking at some of the magazines displaying photographs of me, she began to reveal a deeply moving family history to me: "Your father, my brother—we had a sister named Pearl. She was a beautiful singer, and a beautiful person. But two years before you were born, Pearl died. She lost her life while trying to get rid of an unwanted pregnancy. Pearl died from the procedure.

"And when your mother became pregnant with you outside of wedlock, there were those who were urging her to 'get rid of that baby.' But we sisters rallied due to grief over Pearl. We said, 'We're not going through this again.' And your mother's mother made a trip from the southern part of Trinidad to the northern region, to visit with your father's mother. The two mothers talked for quite a while. They made a pact; they would pray. Their prayer was simply, 'Lord, make this child's life a blessing to the world.' After you were born, I watched our mother continue to pray over your baby bassinet by candlelight, 'Make this child's life a blessing.'"

My aunt's visit and what she told me still brings tears to my eyes. God helped me before I was born. My aunt Pearl died; I was able to live. I am the result of—and what anyone has seen in my life is—God's answer to two grandmothers' prayers. And I realize God knew me in the womb and that He was my help long before birth. Just like He says He knows all of us before we're born (Jeremiah 1:5).

I was born into a troubled situation. My parents' intimacy before their marriage was not endorsed by God. Too often that kind of relationship does not endure. If ever there is a blessing, it is in marriage. My wife has been the source of my greatest support. While virtuous character is the foundation on which a Christian home is built—my family's foundation was cracked. My parents had such a rough go.

I have a saying that God gave to me: It is in the quiet crucible of our personal, private sufferings that our noblest dreams are born and God's greatest gifts are given; and often God gives His greatest gifts in compensation for what we have endured and what we have been through. I can look back and see how God was guiding me into His plans for me.

God helped me long before I began traveling the world; before I came into relationship with six US presidents; before a hug and a thank you from Mother Teresa for singing "Amazing Grace"; before singing of grace in the presence of Israel's Prime Minister Rabin and Palestinian leader Yasser Arafat. There's no one I could have ever wanted to meet that God has not allowed me to meet in the course of my life, while singing during a worldwide itinerary.

When I was five or six years old, I would imagine meeting people all over the world. I had a little red tricycle and I would turn it on its side and spin the front wheel, and sit there for hours, and I would dream . . . I was flying. When our family emigrated from Trinidad to Canada, my father used to take us to the airport, and I would grab a handful of luggage tags when no one was looking, just dreaming about where I would travel. I would close the door of my room and dream.

Later, when I was invited to attend a Christian school near Toronto in my last year of high school, I prayed for the first time, "Whatever you want me to do I'll do. But God I'd like to travel. Let me travel."

In college, one of my instructors told me, "Why don't you do what God wants you to do, not what you want to do?" A day passed, and two men came up to me and said they wanted me to travel to do evangelism. The next few days, I walked the campus in a daze. That's when I began to listen, and for the first time heard God speak to my heart. *I've seen your dreams. Give me your dreams and I will let you glimpse the dreams I'm dreaming for you. I will take you to sing for the masses and I want you to be prepared to speak truth to people of influence and power.* Little did I know then that in giving my life to the Lord, I would live the dream God had been dreaming for me.

It's as though He heard those prayers from those two grandmothers and said, I'm going to help this child. He placed in my throat an instrument that has been my help, and that He has used to help countless millions of people. I can't begin to tell you the stories of peoples' lives touched and helped because of God's dream for me. I've been to Africa. I've been to Parliament. I have circumnavigated the world. God's given me a motto: you don't have to compromise to be recognized. The only singing I do is singing for Him.

Once I went to a hospital to visit a dear lady who had been struggling. As I walked down the hall to see her, a man came up to me and said, "After my son was born at eight months, he went into a coma. A woman gave us a copy of your music and I started playing it for my son every day. He began to improve just listening to your singing! As he grew up, we kept playing your music. I want you to know that 10 years later, he came out of that coma and he lived to age 17. I believe God used your music in his life." God allowed me to live His dream, to live the dreams He placed in my heart, and then He used the gift to be a help with people I will never know, and never see until I see the kingdom.

One day, I was on a train to Philadelphia. I approached the seat of a man camped out with his papers and briefcase across the seat. I could sense his lowness and darkness, like he needed the Lord. I asked if the seat next to him was taken. He said no and he smiled. It was Chuck Colson, who went to prison for Watergate, and who afterward dedicated the rest of his life to prisoners and their families. He would later take me with him into the prisons. He would speak and I would sing. On his board of directors, I watched and learned how to build a ministry of integrity.

It was brought to our attention the children of those who are in prison; an opportunity for us to bring help and support to these children. I began to research what would be the best thing we could do. I found out how to increase the density of helping, caring adults in their life orbit and to bring them Christian education, with interactive support. We began to build US Dream Academy. Founded about 20 years ago, we now also provide tutoring and mentoring to parents whose children are incarcerated.

Having the access to people of influence and people of great net worth and trying to leverage that access into help for children whose parents are in prison has been one of the most exiting and rewarding experiences of my life. I never dreamed I could use music in this way.

I once went to hear an old Black evangelist preach and they were reading his long list of accomplishments. He had his eyes closed and his hand on his chin and he was rocking back and forth and patting his feet and when he got up to speak he soared in his anointing. I deduced his preflight "checklist."

After that, before I performed, I would likewise enter into the foundation of all of my blessings: I went "to the mountain before I went to the multitude." It has been wonderful to depend upon that spiritual power—not just depend on the talent or skill, or those deciding whether you will be heard, but on God, the source of power itself.

Dr. E. E. Cleveland taught me about going to God. He taught me to seek to be a blessing to the world. He said one day, "I've learned how to pray every hour on the hour." I began trying to do so too. It's not easy. I would buy watches designed to alarm every hour so I could stop and pray. After a few years, I did not need the watches. I learned how important it is to buttress and strengthen with daily, hourly, secret prayer—talking to God all through the day (1 Thessalonians 5:16–22).

I began asking God, *how can we use technology to accelerate time with You; praying every hour on the hour?* God gave us an app for cellphones, called Divine Alerts, that allows you to set the frequency of delivery and every hour you can receive a Scripture from the Psalms and you can walk through a chapter in the Bible. Every hour an inspirational word or thought from God. And I have been using it; it's been an incredible blessing. There is a divine sparkle that we can only get from communion with God.

A lifetime of dependence on Him, sparked by two praying grandmothers. I am grateful.

An Invitation

Diane Proctor Reeder

This is what the LORD Almighty says: "Consider
now! Call for the wailing women to come."
JEREMIAH 9:17 NIV

The African nation of Liberia was in the midst of civil war
in the year 2000. Three years later, Christian social worker
Leymah Gbowee, deciding that enough was enough (or in the
words of Fannie Lou Hamer, deciding she was "sick and tired
of being sick and tired"), recruited hundreds of Christian
women to pray. They strategically placed themselves in view
of the home of Liberian President Charles Taylor and watched
as his motorcade passed them daily. And they prayed. And
they wrote and publicly presented him with a position statement. And they prayed. They surrounded public buildings,
sat on lawns. And they prayed. They took some unorthodox
actions. And they prayed.

A few short months later, peacekeeping talks began along
with disarmament. The women continued their spiritual and
on-the-ground activity.

Gbowee would go on to win the Nobel Peace Prize along
with Liberia's first female president, Ellen Johnson Sirleaf.

Women hold a special place in God's kingdom as influ-
encers. It is an historic position that dates back to antiquity.
The prophet Jeremiah spoke forth God's Word when His own
chosen people were steeped in idolatry and sin, and he called
for the women to come (Jeremiah 9:17–26).

Come, women
Come and wail.
You know. You know. You know.

I am the only man that wails here.
But the Lord wants to teach wailing,
and you women are cunning,
and you know.

You have lost children
to the violent hordes
and husbands
to strange women.

You have seen your dwelling places
ransacked and in disrepair.
You have walked through ruins, fingered grief in
each shard of bruised memory

The Lord has need of you,
O women who mourn.
You are close to His heart.

For He too
has seen the death of children
(For as in Adam all died)
and the wandering of a spouse
who spurned His embrace
for tongues of wood
and bodies of silver.

Come, women
You know grief.
You know sorrow.

Make haste.
As you pull out your own tears,
cry for all of us.

Maybe it is not too late.
Maybe our tears will turn His heart—
Or why else would He ask you to come?

Come. Come. Make haste.
You know. You know. You know.

In our communities, we face similar challenges with personal as well as institutional violence, challenges that call for a similar response. The mothers of those who have been felled by violence are wailing. We need to wail with them.

REFLECTION:
Study the strategy of the women of Liberia. How were they able to make such an impact? How can we in Black America adapt those lessons to the challenges that we face as well?

Suggested Scripture Reading: Jeremiah 9

Redemption & Memory

Diane Proctor Reeder

*Remember your Creator in the days of your
youth.*

Ecclesiastes 12:1 NIV

The angel of mercy guarded
the tree with fire
and so Adam remembered
their transgression
(Genesis 3:24)

Jacob built an altar to remember
(like Abraham his father)
fought with God
and was turned into Israel
(Genesis 35:7)

The nation Israel took up 12 smooth stones
and remembered miracle
(Joshua 4:6–9)

Israel made God's words
to hang on necks and hands
and their children remembered
(Deuteronomy 6:8)

My aunt saved articles and coins and pictures and we remember heritage and history.

My grandfather recited a poem about a boy's sacrifice:

Little Jack killed on the railroad tracks saving a baby
and we remember love

The memory infuses bone and sinew and skin
it fills our gray matter and irises and mouths and hearts

the memory of sin
the memory of hope
the memory of holiness
the memory of God
that lights every birth.

Topical Index

Scripture Index

Permissions

Enjoy this book? Help us get the word out!

Share a link to the book or
mention it on social media

Write a review on your blog, on a retailer site,
or on our website (dhp.org)

Pick up another copy to share with someone

Recommend this book for your
church, book club, or small group

Follow Discovery House on
social media and join the discussion

Contact us to share your thoughts:

 @discoveryhouse    @DiscoveryHouse

Discovery House
P.O. Box 3566
Grand Rapids, MI 49501 USA

Phone: 1-800-653-8333
Email: books@dhp.org
Web: dhp.org